John Russell, CBE,
has been on the staff of *The New York Times*
since 1974 and was its chief art critic from 1982 till 1990.
From 1949 till 1974 he was art critic of *The Sunday Times*
in London where he organized major exhibitions of
Modigliani, Rouault and Balthus at the Tate Gallery. In
1969 he was co-organizer of 'Pop Art Redefined' at the
Hayward Gallery, and in 1971 he organized an exhibition
of Vuillard for museums in Toronto, Chicago and San
Francisco. He is a member of the American Academy of
Arts and Letters. His numerous publications include
Francis Bacon, published in the World of Art, *The Meanings
of Modern Art*, *Reading Russell*, *Paris* and *London*, and
monographs on Vuillard, Matisse, Max Ernst,
Henry Moore and Ben Nicholson.

WORLD OF ART

This famous series
provides the widest available
range of illustrated books on art in all its aspects.
If you would like to receive a complete list
of titles in print please write to:
THAMES AND HUDSON
30 Bloomsbury Street, London WC1B 3QP
In the United States please write to:
THAMES AND HUDSON INC.
500 Fifth Avenue, New York, New York 10110

Printed in Singapore

Seurat

John Russell

225 illustrations
52 in color

Thames and Hudson

To Véra Vladimirovna

© 1965 Thames and Hudson Ltd, London

Published in the United States of America in 1985
by Thames and Hudson Inc., 500 Fifth Avenue,
New York, New York 10110
Reprinted 1997

Library of Congress Catalog Card Number 85-51234
ISBN 0-500-20032-7

Printed and bound in Singapore

Contents

Page 7 Preface

9 CHAPTER ONE
Background and Beginnings

65 CHAPTER TWO
Seurat the Draughtsman

115 CHAPTER THREE
The First of the Great Pictures

141 CHAPTER FOUR
The Pan-Athenaic Frieze Brought Up to Date

197 CHAPTER FIVE
Master-Subjects In and Out of Doors

249 CHAPTER SIX
A Career Cut Short

271 Short Bibliography

273 List of Illustrations

283 Index

Preface

This book could not have appeared at all, in its present form, without the kindness and constant support of M. César de Hauke, whose two-volume catalogue is now the indispensable point of departure for all students of Seurat. Drawings and paintings referred to in the book but not illustrated are identified by their number in this catalogue, which follows the picture title in brackets. Not only was M. de Hauke good enough to let me consult this catalogue in proof-stage, but he made available a high proportion of the photographs which have been used for the illustrations of this book. The publishers wish to join me in thanking M. de Hauke for a gesture which has made it possible, for the first time, to present a panoramic survey of Seurat's achievement in one volume.

Professor John Rewald was generous enough to answer a number of questions which I put to him at various times; and Mr Henri Dorra, Mr Frederick Sweet and Mr Louis Pomerantz also put themselves out on my behalf. When Mr Robert L. Herbert was in London I benefited by his conversation as much as I had benefited before, and have benefited since, by his writings. At a late stage in the book's preparation Mr Benedict Nicolson was kind enough not only to read the manuscript, but to lend me relevant papers dating from his acquaintance with Félix Fénéon.

It goes without saying that none of these people is in any way responsible for whatever shortcomings the book may have.

J. R.

CHAPTER ONE

Background and Beginnings

To burst upon the world at the age of twenty-four with a painting that will one day hang on equal terms with Piero and Poussin is an ambition from which even the most sanguine might draw back in modesty.

Yet Seurat achieved just this when, on 15th May 1884, the inaugural Salon des Artistes Indépendants was opened in a disused post-office building on the site of the burnt-out Palais des Tuileries, and anyone who strayed into the bar could find there an enormous painting called *Une Baignade, Asnières* (*Ill. 127*). This canvas now dominates the nineteenth-century rooms in the National Gallery in London as an undisputed keywork in European art. But at the time very few people took note of it. It had been refused by the jury of the official Salon of 1884, where the picture of the year was Armand Dumaresq's *Lecture de l'Annuaire de la Cavalerie*, and the hanging committee of the Indépendants thought it either too unwieldy (it measures 79 inches by 118) or too eccentric for the exhibition rooms proper. And yet no début could have been grander or more auspicious; for at the very outset of his exhibiting career Seurat had established himself, outright, as the kinsman and the peer of the great picture-architects of the past.

It would be the wildest romancing to suppose that a picture like the *Baignade* results from anything but the most careful and elaborate preparation. Not only was the final version preceded by a great deal of preliminary experiment (fourteen sketches in oils exist for the *Baignade*, and there are ten related drawings) but the capacity to attempt such a picture at all, in the years 1883–4, implies a sustained and prodigious effort of knowledge, will-power, meditation and historical sense. That the *Baignade* should have been painted by a man barely twenty-four years old, who had never before

1 A copy, dating from Seurat's sixteenth year, of a figure in Poussin's *Ordination*. Seurat knew this painting from an engraving, and not from the original (which was then in Bridgewater House and now belongs to the Duke of Sutherland)

2 Another drawing from Seurat's first year at art-school: a version, this time, of a group of horsemen from the Parthenon frieze. Like nearly all Seurat's drawings from the antique, it was made from a cast

shown a painting in public, is a miracle: a miracle not of 'inspiration' but of reason, and tenacity, and profound poetic impulse.

When Seurat came, in 1884–6, to paint the *Grande Jatte*, and even more so when in the remaining years of the 1880s he painted *Les Poseuses*, *La Parade*, *Le Chahut* and *Le Cirque*, he was in increasing degree a Parisian figure. But up till May 1884 he and his work were known only to a very small group of personal friends. And as his was the most private of natures we know almost nothing of what he was thinking and feeling at that time. All that he would say in later years was: 'I painted like that because I wanted to get through to something new—a kind of painting that was my own.'

3 This drawing of *Ulysses and the Suitors* is one of many which belonged to Seurat's admirer and champion, Félix Fénéon. Dated 1876, it is marked by a neo-classical idiom which Seurat probably picked up while studying the engravings of Flaxman

We do, on the other hand, know of the sketches for the *Baignade* (*Chap. 3*); and of about eighty other unrelated small oils dated between 1882 and 1884; and recent research has revealed a total of several hundred drawings anterior to Seurat's début at the Indépendants. It is therefore clear that when he chose to make that début as the author of a very large and entirely magisterial canvas he had already behind him a long private history of experiment.

The critic's job is to fit that history together, and a great deal has been done to that end in the last twenty years. But a brief survey, as good as any of its successors, was contributed to the *Revue Blanche* in 1899 by Paul Signac, who has been a colleague of Seurat's and one of his closest and most admiring friends. This is what he says of the origins of Seurat's style:

'Seurat was a student of the Ecole des Beaux-Arts; but he was preserved from the dismal influence of that School by his intelligence, his strength of will, his lucid and methodical turn of mind, his uncontaminated taste and his painterly eye. Constantly in and out of the museums, prizing our libraries for their stocks of art-books and engravings, he drew from the study of the classical masters just the strength that he needed to stand out against the lessons of the School. In the course of these independent studies, he noticed that in Rubens, as in Raphael, and in Michelangelo as in Delacroix, line and chiaro-scuro and colour and composition were subject to analogous laws: rhythm, proportion and contrast.

4 Another drawing of 1876: *The Separation*. Seurat's vision of the ancient world owes much, once again, to the linear example of Flaxman, but a related tradition runs from Ingres, Chassériau and Puvis de Chavannes to the *Young Spartans* (1860) of Degas

5 Mr William I. Homer has identified the sculpture from which this drawing was made, between 1876 and 1878, as a *St Martha*, of the School of Troyes, dated around 1510

'The traditions of the Far East and the writings of Chevreul, Charles Blanc, Humbert de Superville, d'O. N. Rood, and H. Helmholtz were also of use to him. For a long time he analysed the work of Delacroix, and had no difficulty in finding in it the application of traditional laws, alike in colour and line, and he saw clearly what still had to be done to complete the forms of progress glimpsed by the Romantic master.

6 Professor R. L. Herbert suggests that in this drawing of *c.* 1877. Seurat was working from a cast of the Hellenistic figure of a satyr and goat which is now in Madrid. He could also have seen, in the Louvre, a seventeenth-century bronze after the original

'Seurat's studies resulted in his well-considered and fertile theory of contrasts: a theory to which all his work was thereafter subjected. He applied it first to chiaroscuro: with the simplest of resources, the white of a sheet of Ingres paper and the black of a Conté crayon, skilfully graded or contrasted, he executed some four hundred drawings, the most beautiful painters' drawings in existence. And then, having achieved mastery of contrasts of tone, he tackled colour in the same way and, from 1882 onwards, applied to colour the same laws of contrast and painted with elements clearly distinguished from one another—admittedly he did tone down his colours—without having been influenced by the impressionists, whose very existence was unknown to him at the time.'

We might now fault this in detail. It is not quite true, for instance, that 'the very existence' of the Impressionists was unknown to Seurat at any time after May 1879, when he went to the fourth Impressionist exhibition and saw the work of Degas, Monet and Pissarro. But in general Signac's sketch of his friend's first years as a painter can still stand.

One or two facts can be added to it. Georges Seurat was born on 2nd December 1859, in a little street in the tenth arrondissement of Paris.

His father, Chrysostome-Antoine Seurat (*Ill. 7*), was a minor legal official, a *huissier*, with an office near La Villette; and to this steadily lucrative occupation Seurat the painter owed the competence which meant that, unlike his friend Pissarro, he never had to worry about money.

Seurat's father came from Champagne; his mother, born Ernestine Faivre, was Parisian. He inherited, therefore, a northerly orientation: and this he kept to throughout his short life, claiming that nowhere could there be a light more congenial than that of Asnières, on the outskirts of Paris, taking his working holidays on the coast between Cherbourg and Le Havre, and never to our knowledge putting a foot south of Pontaubert (Yonne).

He was a classic northerner; exact, taciturn, persevering, slow to make up his mind but method personified when once the decision was taken.

7 It is very possible that in this drawing, dated *c.* 1884, of a man seated reading on a terrace Seurat used his father as the model

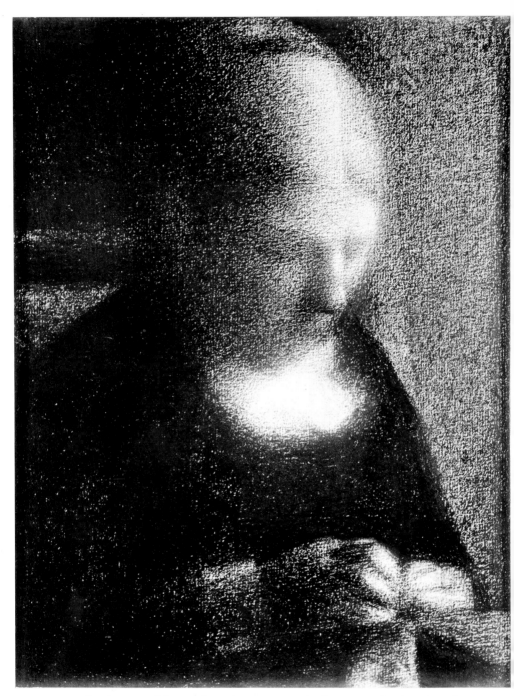

8 This drawing of the artist's mother was rejected when sent in for the Salon of 1883: it is now in the Metropolitan Museum, New York

9 M. de Hauke believes this portrait, also dated *c.* 1883, to be of Madame Seurat. Like the preceding illustration, it foreshadows the *intimiste* subjects of Vuillard

To his mother (*Ills. 8, 9*) Seurat owed, first, the example of an unvarying and provident affection; and, second, the experience in childhood of what was to be one of the grand preoccupations of his art: the lower-class Parisian pleasure-ground. Shortly after his birth the family moved from the *triste* and crapulous rue de Bondy to 110 Boulevard de Magenta. From there it was an easy walk to the Parc des Buttes-Chaumont, which was opened in Seurat's eighth year and presented, then as now, the image of a poor man's paradise, with lakes, grottoes, temples, manageable mountains and a great range of simple distractions. These metropolitan pleasures, and the variety and oddity of the people who came to enjoy

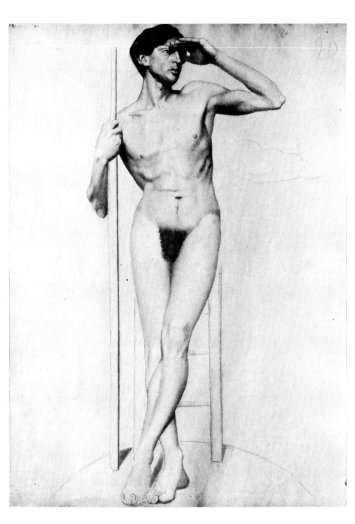

10 A life-drawing
dated *c.* 1877. Many
of the models em-
ployed by the little
municipal school
were drawn from the
dregs of local human-
ity, but in this case
Seurat gave the living
figure something of
the antique grandeur
of the later *Une
Baignade, Asnières*

them, were to remain with Seurat until his death; and from their
riverside equivalents he was to assemble the material for two great
masterpieces: *Une Baignade, Asnières* and *Un Dimanche d'Eté à l'Ile de
la Grande Jatte (Ill. 133).* Seurat's mother commissioned a painting
from Pissarro in 1886 (the year of Seurat's *Grande Jatte*); but as far as a
taste for modern painting is concerned the impulse seems more likely
to have come from her son and his friends than from within herself.

From his father, Seurat's inheritances were more complex. Method
was the first among them: Seurat senior was exact, firm, set-faced

11 Comparable, as Mr Herbert suggests, to the youthful work of Holbein or
Dürer, this drawing (1878–9) of an aged Hindu is as remarkable for its stringent
observation as for Seurat's tender and compassionate handling of bodily frailties

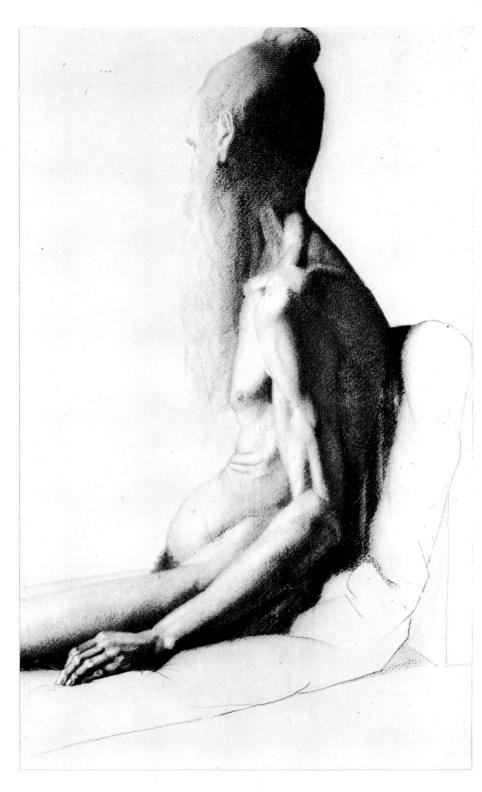

12 Seurat knew Holbein's portrait of Sir Richard Southwell after an oil copy in the Louvre, and not from the original in the Uffizi. This drawing of *c.* 1877–8 formerly belonged to the poet Paul Eluard

in all he did, and he insisted on the dignities, such as they were, of his office. ('The notary', was Degas' nickname for Seurat the painter, and it related as much to his bearing as to the sobriety of his dress.) Obstacles put in the way of Seurat *père* were quietly overcome. He had had, for instance, the misfortune to lose his right arm in an accident: from his sleeve there protruded, thereafter, an iron hook with which he made himself remarkably adept. (Not only could he carve a leg of lamb but he could distribute it, slice by faultless slice, on the end of his hook.) He was by nature secret and solitary (traits which his son inherited at full strength); and as it was not easy to indulge these inclinations in Paris, he took a little house at Le Raincy, some seven miles due east of the family apartment, and lived there by himself for a great part of the year. Le Raincy in the 1860s had still a certain look of the aristocratic estate, formerly the property of the Duc d'Orléans, which had been parcelled out as recently as 1852.

The neighbourhood gave Seurat some of his first and most abrupt and informal landscape-subjects; but quite as important as this was his father's habit of collecting popular religious prints. These were present in great numbers both in the Boulevard de Magenta, among the massive mahogany Louis-Philippe furniture, and in the rustications of Le Raincy. Many came from Mame, in Tours; others from the famous house of Pellerin, in Epinal. Seurat senior was deeply religious—to the extent, even, of going through a form of Mass in the basement of his little house at Le Raincy, with the gardener to serve him—and although we know nothing of Seurat's own convictions there is no doubt that the daily experience of popular imagery had a deep effect upon him. Robert L. Herbert tells us that at his death 'sixty-one pieces of *imagerie populaire*, primitive broadsides dating largely from the 1840s' were found in his studio; these must have shown him, already in childhood, how to simplify an image and give it an abrupt, monumental quality; and recollections of them pushed their way into the most complex of all his paintings, the *Grande Jatte*. Altogether, therefore, he owed his father a great deal: financial independence, a passion for solitude and isolation, and a belief in the primacy of the image among means of communication.

Herbert reproduces a drawing dating from Seurat's eighth, ninth or tenth year which has certain affinities with his mature style; but in general he was not thought to be at all precocious, either at his first municipal drawing school, where Justin Lequien was his teacher, or at the Ecole des Beaux-Arts, where he arrived in the winter of 1877–8. In the examiners' terms he was a docile, industrious but quite ungifted student; in reality he was making the fullest use of his exceptional intellectual curiosity. In class he might, in March 1879, be only forty-seventh out of about eighty; but in the range and force of his researches he was a man on his own. It was not then as easy as it is today to have access to the full range of the art of other times and other countries, and Seurat often drew not from the originals, but from copies or reproductions of the things he admired (*Ills. 1, 2*). He was always in and out of the Louvre, where he spent as much time in the Egyptian and Assyrian rooms as in the sections devoted to painting. A natural bookman, he built up a Musée Imaginaire of his own nearly seventy years before Malraux invented the phrase. And he had the run of that most curious conglomeration, the group of casts and copies in the chapel of the Ecole des Beaux-Arts. Already in 1877 he had made a beautiful drawing of the Ilissus from the Parthenon frieze, and the artists after whom he made drawings in the next few years were to include Raphael, Holbein (*Ill. 12*), Ingres (*Ill. 13*), Poussin (*Ill. 1*), Puget, Ghiberti, Giovanni Bellini, Perugino, Michelangelo, Titian and Pontormo. It can be argued that the copies after Piero della Francesca in the chapel of the Ecole des Beaux-Arts were especially useful to him. (These copies had been commissioned by Charles Blanc from a painter called Loyaux, and they form part of a large collection of copies and casts which can still be seen in the chapel). He also drew from antique sculptures, some of them familiar from casts in the Ecole des Beaux-Arts, others accessible in the Louvre. But Henri Lehmann, his master at the Beaux-Arts, was a pupil of Ingres, and it was Ingres above all whom Seurat favoured at this time (*Ill. 13*).

The best of Seurat's drawings after the Old Masters, or from the antique, have a gravity and equanimity which make them, in effect, a sublime variant of art-criticism. Herbert is clearly correct in saying

13 Seurat in this life-drawing of *c*. 1876 was looking back to the Ingres of *La Source* and *Venus Anadyoneme*; but anatomical truth was holding its own against Ingres' idealized suavity

that the simplifications of the central figure in *Les Poseuses* (*Ill. 187*) can be related back to drawings made as early as 1875–6. But in general neither the classroom-drawings nor his earliest paintings suggest the final direction of his gifts. Neither in style nor in subject was there any distinct foreshadowing until, in November 1880, Seurat returned from a year's military service and re-established himself in Paris. (Foreseeing in all things, Seurat had exploited the system by which it was possible, after passing an examination and paying 1,500 francs to the State, to serve one year, instead of three, in the army.)

It has become traditional to say that during his term of service at Brest (*Ills. 14, 15*) Seurat became aware of his destiny as a painter of *marines*: or more exactly, as Sir Kenneth Clark puts it, that: 'The revelation of light came to him as he gazed on the sea during the hours of sentry-duty.' This may be true; but the facts are that Seurat did not attempt to paint the sea until the summer of 1885 at Grandcamp, and that in the drawings to which he gave so much of his time between

14 This page from the Brest notebook constitutes the earliest of Seurat's surviving drawings of the sea-coast, and dates from his year in the army (1879–80)

15 Another page from the Brest notebook: figures studied in outline only, in the manner of a frieze and brought up close to the picture-plane

1879 and 1882 the sea plays almost no part. Far more important, to my mind, than his first contacts with the sea was the emergence, within two years of his leaving the Ecole des Beaux-Arts, of nearly all the themes he was to employ five, six, seven and eight years later in his major oil-paintings. These themes appeared not in his oils, of which the earliest are Ingresque in subject, but in his drawings.

There were several reasons why this should be so. To begin with, the nature and objects of painting were themselves in question at this time. This may seem a curious point of view to those who remember that in 1881 Manet painted *Le Bar aux Folies-Bergère* and Renoir *Le Déjeuner des Canotiers*. An aesthetic of pure instinct could have no greater monuments than these two. But that aesthetic was already in dissolution. The Impressionist group, as a group, had virtually ceased to exist. ('To keep in with that Jew Pissarro means revolution,' said Renoir in 1882.) Manet was a dying man. Renoir, by 1883, was

16, 17 Soon after his return to Paris Seurat perfected, in metropolitan studies like the two on this page, the technique of drawing in
summary outline which he had begun to master in Brest. To the left
is *Un Bonhomme;* below, the marvellously characterized bootblack
who is one of the high-points in Seurat's early career as a draughts-
man. Both drawings are dated *c.* 1881

18 Three years later, in this drawing of a boy standing near a lamp, Seurat was perfecting a totally different mode of expression: one in which single and anonymous figures are blacked in against a minimum of metropolitan furniture and with a horizon-line set, as here, mysteriously high

convinced that he himself had 'gone to the end of Impressionism and . . . didn't know either how to paint or to draw'. Even Pissarro, the white knight of the movement, was convinced by 1883 that some radical change was needed. The time called, in short, for a shift away from the instinctual procedures of Impressionism towards a more orderly, rational, disciplined, scientific approach. This is the problem to which we should relate Cézanne's wish to make of Impressionism 'something solid and lasting, like museum-art'.

It was not, however, a crisis which necessarily presented itself in these terms to Seurat and his friends at the outset of their careers. Not until 1882 did Impressionism have any direct influence on Seurat; and meanwhile he had quite other enthusiasms. Of one of these we have an equivocal souvenir in one of his earliest paintings: the *Pierre Puvisse* [sic] *de Chavannes* (*Ill. 19*). This is a variant of *Le Pauvre Pêcheur*, which Puvis painted in 1881 and showed in the Salon in the same year: Seurat was clearly quick off the mark in making his variant of it, though he can hardly have been as quick as is suggested by the date (*c.* 1879–80) which was once attributed to the painting. But the fact that he pounced on the picture is indicative of his preoccupation with Puvis.

That preoccupation may seem baffling to our own generation; for of all the consequential painters of the French nineteenth century, none has sunk lower in popular esteem than Puvis de Chavannes. His work is not so much discounted as ignored. Not one of his paintings is available in colour-reproduction—or so it would seem from the UNESCO catalogue of such things—and the enthusiast is rare who seeks out his big decorations in the Panthéon or the Sorbonne, let alone the Musée de Lyon or the Public Library in Boston, Mass. Puvis has gone to the bottom, though he may soon rise again. Yet in the mid-1880s, when Seurat was at the height of his powers, few artists were so highly regarded by the intelligent layman: Seurat's close friend Gustave Kahn made this point when he said later that 'Puvis was the major painter as to whose merits we were most nearly unanimous. With his integrity, his noble ambition, and his new and delicate sense of harmony, he was beyond and above discussion.'

30

19 Perhaps the oddest of Seurat's early oil-paintings is this one, in which a variant of Puvis de Chavannes' *Pauvre Pêcheur* has been set out in the open air: conceivably there was a point, now lost to us, in the contrasting of Puvis' landscape-practice with Seurat's own

If very little of this remains, it is partly because later painters adapted the sweet marrow of Puvis' artistic personality for their own purposes and left the bones to moulder. Seurat, for instance, was able to articulate and democratize and make monumental elements which in Puvis himself were stilted and arthritic. Picasso in his blue period brought a vivid and informal poetry to themes which Puvis left stranded in sentimentality. In our own country Augustus John in his large decorations adapted Puvis so deftly to the English taste that when people tried to track down his sources the nerve of curiosity was already cut. And though people know, in examinees' terms, that Gauguin and Maillol both copied Puvis they regard the fact as a historical oddity. (Thomas Couture today stands even lower than Puvis; but Couture—probably at the time of his exhibition in 1880—was a painter from whom Seurat learnt something about the nature of colour.)

20 (*left*) A favourite Parisian subject of Seurat's was that of a solitary figure leaning on the parapet of the Seine: this drawing of *c.* 1881 announced, also, the theme of tree-trunks

21 (*above*) This drawing of 1881 is the earliest of the many studies which Seurat made of itinerant entertainers

22 This portrait of his friend and colleague Aman-Jean was the first and only work by Seurat to be accepted by the official Salon: it was shown there in 1883

Puvis the man has gone down with Puvis the artist, but he too deserves better treatment. From his self-portrait in the Uffizi (not, again, the easiest picture in the world to see) one might take him for an imposing old fossil: clear of brow, certainly, and with old-fashioned grand good looks, but fatally a part of art's officialdom, with his high stiff white collar, his frock-coat firmly buttoned and the rosette of the Légion d'Honneur precisely in place. Yet this would be an injustice. Puvis was thirty-six years older than Seurat, at a time when differences of age counted for much, but to Seurat and his friends he was not simply a friendly and conversable old buffer. He had, to begin with, a fine record of independence and discernment. He had got on to Degas in 1863 and to Bazille in 1869. He was to be one of the artists who subscribed to buy Manet's *Olympia* for the Louvre. He was a friend of Berthe Morisot and had employed Suzanne Valadon as a model. He had never tried to push his own kind of painting, and in life he had none of the wan and wistful characteristics of his art. (He even put that art to ribald uses: the Goncourt *Journal* of 1862 described him as having knocked up some hilarious scenery for an evening of amateur theatricals at Théophile Gautier's.) For years he was chairman of a monthly dinner of painters, sculptors, musicians and men of letters, at which his high good humour, his robust common sense and his easy sociability set the tone of the evening.

Seurat and his close friend Aman-Jean (*Ill. 22*) went often to Puvis' studio in the Place Pigalle. The old gentleman had big decorations on hand at the time, and the canvases were stretched up the wall and allowed to overflow on to the floor for easier management. Aman-Jean remembered Puvis as a lordly, fine-spoken and sharply observant old person who made the two young visitors welcome. Soon he was setting them to work to square up his sketches and generally help him to get the heavy work under way: the master would discourse the while, from the top of his tall ladder, on Greece and on the notion of art. The date of these regular visits remains uncertain: Aman-Jean's son, in his recent book of memoirs, speaks of his father having seen 'the Panthéon frescoes [*sic*] in the studio in 1884 or thereabouts', but as the Panthéon decorations were erected in 1876 this must be a

23 (*above*) This small version of Puvis de Chavannes' *Doux Pays* was acquired not long ago by the Yale University Art Gallery: it is one of many paintings by Puvis which foreshadow elements in Seurat's *Une Baignade, Asnières* and *Un Dimanche Après-Midi à l'Ile de la Grande Jatte*

24 (*right*) *Cheval Noir et Personnages*, a preliminary sketch by Seurat for the *Baignade* (*Ill. 127*), and one whose organization derives, however obliquely, from Puvis

miscalculation. Aman-Jean's friendship with Seurat was at its closest before November 1879, when Seurat went off to do his military service, and after his return from the army a year later. (A pencil-portrait of Aman-Jean, *Ill. 22*, sent to the Salon of 1883, was Seurat's first exhibited work.) It seems at least probable that Seurat knew Puvis at the time when the older artist was at work on the enormous decoration, *Ludus Pro Patria*, which was completed for the Salon of 1882, and that he may also have been in on the preparation of *Doux Pays* (*Ill. 23*), which was shown to the public at the same time.

25, 26 Two examples of the tenebrous country-subjects which Seurat perfected, partly under the influence of J.-F. Millet, in *c.* 1883: 25 (*above*), *Le Labourage*, 26 (*below*), *Les Deux Charrettes*

From Puvis, and in particular from these two major works, Seurat could have acquired several items in the repertory of images in his own two great riverside canvases. The hushed and still world of *Doux Pays* has often been linked to Seurat, and it is certainly true that Seurat took to heart the scudding white sails, the details of disembarkation, the disposition of seated and reclining figures, the frieze-like groupings and the lyrical fragments of still-life which turn up in one after another of Puvis' works.

But not only was Puvis pure gold as a companion and as a source of rewarding images. He stood for an attitude to art which had lapsed, and which it was Seurat's as yet unfocused ambition to revive. Painting stood, as Puvis saw it, for the establishment of a moral order among experiences. It was a comment upon society,

27 *Cavalier sur une Route*, a drawing of *c.* 1883 in which Seurat once again explores the atmospheric possibilities of twilight

not a chaos of subjective impressions. History-pieces like the *Charles-Martel* of 1873 and religious pieces like the *Prodigal Son* of 1878–9 did not satisfy this ambition directly, but it was realized to the limit of Puvis' capacities in the works which came to fruition around the time that Seurat knew him.

Puvis painted these pictures when the tide was at last turning his way. Realism on the one hand and Impressionism on the other were grinding, as it then seemed, to a halt. 'We had had enough', a critic wrote later, 'of so-called veracity, and of that blinding colour with which people had tried to stun us. We wanted dreams, emotion, poetry. We were tired of light that was too vivid and too crude, and the misty and poetical art of Puvis summoned forth all our devotion.' Strindberg the painter-dramatist was in Paris in 1885, the year after Seurat had shown the *Baignade*. 'Naturalism is at its last gasp,' he

28 In *Le Cheval au Tombereau*, again of *c.* 1883, Seurat makes an everyday farm-cart rear up against the sky like some monumental survivor from pre-history

29 *Paysans aux Champs, c.* 1883: the subtly curving tree at the extreme right is one of Seurat's most characteristic compositional touches; in the outline of men, horse, and cart, and in the broadly shelving foreground there is, once again, a formalized and antique grandeur

wrote, 'but one name excites universal admiration: that of Puvis de Chavannes.' Nor was all this simply a matter of presentation. Puvis stood for a radical change in the intentions of art. The thing directly seen no longer sufficed: what people wanted was the thing purified and re-born after lengthy reflection and in accordance with a coherent moral idea of the world. (Brunetière said of Puvis that 'The imitation of Nature cannot be the be-all and end-all of painting.')

This was Seurat's own programme, and there is no doubt that knowing Puvis helped him to formulate it. Where he could not follow Puvis was in the self-conscious archaizing, as it now seems to us, of Puvis' imaginary world. It was all very well for a poet like Charles Morice to speak of Puvis as 'a gentle genius exiled in our iron century': Seurat knew, even if he never said it, that Puvis' idea of the Golden Age was to take a lot of casts from the antique and serve them up with wigs on. He saw it as the painter's job to take the iron century on its own terms and make of it something that would challenge Antiquity. But in making the most of what Puvis had to give he manifested intelligence of the highest order. Toulouse-Lautrec's parody of Puvis' *Bois Sacré*, painted in 1885, has an element of superior farce to which Seurat could not have attained, and might indeed not have wished to attain: even today there is an irresistible hilarity in the effect created by Toulouse-Lautrec as we

30 *Au Travail de la Terre, c.* 1883, is one of the first of the drawings in which Seurat took over where Courbet, in his *Stone-Breakers* of 1850, left off

31 *L'Homme à la Pioche, c.* 1883: a theme also treated by Seurat in several of his small early oil-panels

track across from the burlesqued Prodigal Son on the left to the group of figures in modern dress (Lautrec himself among them) on the right. But Seurat's was the method of the genuine inventor; and although Paul Alexis got the thing upside down when he spoke of the *Baignade* as 'a fake Puvis' he did spot a connection which has been obscured for later generations by their indifference to the painter of *Doux Pays*.

While Seurat was working on the many small panels which preceded the sketches for the *Baignade*, he had before him the example not so much of Puvis as of a recent master of Everyday: Jean-François Millet. Direct personal influence was out of the question, since Millet died when Seurat was only sixteen. But

32 *Les Glaneuses* (1857) by Jean-François Millet. In this famous painting from the Louvre can be found not only the motif taken over by Seurat in the painting on the page opposite (*Ill. 33*), but elements also of his pure-landscape practice

engravings of Millet's paintings were easy to come by in Seurat's formative years, and it so happened that Millet came back into the news at just the time when Seurat was ready to profit by his example. Seurat returned to Paris from the army in November 1880, and in March of the following year the *Angélus* was sold for 160,000 francs at auction in Paris. In May 1881 the Hartmann collection of Millet's work was sold up at Hartmann's house in the rue de Courcelles: this offered the chance of seeing some of Millet's grandest and most carefully constructed canvases—among them *Le Greffier*, *Les Batteurs de Sarrazin*, and *Le Printemps*. Again in 1881, the publication of Sensier's book on Millet made it possible for sympathizers to share the memories of an intimate friend and supporter of the artist.

As had happened in the case of Puvis, Seurat derived a part of his repertory of images directly from Millet. Anyone who goes to the top floor of the Louvre will find there Millet's *Les Glaneuses* of 1857 (*Ill. 32*). In this one picture, and in an earlier, independent variant, now in the Museum of Fine Arts, Springfield, Mass., three themes later taken up by Seurat can be identified: the *Paysannes au travail* (*Ill. 33*) who are the subject of a painting in the Guggenheim Museum; the haystacks which Seurat isolated and made monumental (see *Meule de Foin, Ill. 34*); and on to the horizon to the right of the picture the steep roofs half in and half out of the sun which Seurat

33 *Paysannes au Travail, c.* 1883, is one of the first paintings in which Seurat applied the colour-theories of Rood, mingling yellow and orange with the green and giving the orange of the hats a touch or two of its complementary blue

made the principal subject of *Maisons et Jardin* (*Ill. 35*) and *Ville d'Avray, Maisons Blanches* (*Ill. 40*) which is now in the Walker Art Gallery, Liverpool.

But even more important than the kinship of motif, as between Millet and Seurat, was the kinship of minds. Millet is still regarded by many people as primarily a painter of simple-minded pietistic scenes, and the true grandeur of his achievement has been overlaid by the brief success of the *Angélus*. But the truth is that Millet was a lifelong agnostic and a man of immense and varied cultivation. Among the French painters of his time he was second only to Delacroix in this latter respect; and whereas Delacroix inclined more and more, in later life, towards a fastidious conservatism, Millet

34 *La Meule de Foin* (*Haystack*), c. 1883: a characteristic instance of Seurat's ability to simplify and monumentalize a quite ordinary aspect of country life

35 *Maisons et Jardin*, *c.* 1882: a painting in which the sharp-angled and schematized portrayal of roofs and walls carries on from Millet's handling of such things in his *Les Glaneuses*

was open to ideas of every sort. An enthusiastic and retentive reader of Virgil, Theocritus, Milton and La Fontaine, he kept casts from the Parthenon frieze in his studio and, many years before Bonnard and his fellow-Nabis, was a keen admirer of the Japanese print. Without descending into mannerism, he scoured the art of the past for imagery which, when transposed into the environment of everyday country life, would help to confer upon that life the status of epic. He had studied Greek vase-painting, for instance; he had reproductions of Giotto and Fra Angelico in his studio; and he could call on the masters of the European past, from Masaccio to Brueghel, without a touch of archaization. Classical art, the Italian primitives, Dutch and Flemish art, Japanese prints—all contributed to Millet's mature style; but it takes a keen eye to identify them within what seems to most people the epitome of naturalism. In mixing sand with his pigments to get away from the blandishments of *la belle peinture* Millet was once again forty years ahead of his time: but for this also he received no credit.

36 (*above left*) *Vache dans un Pré, c.* 1882, one of the earliest of the small panels in which Seurat experimented with criss-cross brushstrokes. 37 (*left*) A pencil-drawing (*c.* 1883) of clothes drying on a line. 38 (*above*) *Paysanne, les Mains au Sol, c.* 1882, one of the grandest of Seurat's single-figure studies of country-life

39 *Casseur de Pierres* (*Stone-Breaker*), *c.* 1883: something, for once, of conventional modelling, and of traditional chiaroscuro, enters into this drawing

40 *Ville d'Avray, Maisons Blanches*, oil on canvas, *c.* 1882: from the village which had been painted with celestial effect by Corot in the 1850s Seurat took, above all, the flattened horizontals which were to characterize his landscapes right through to the Gravelines series of 1890

Millet, as much as Puvis, was necessary to Seurat at this stage in his career, and it is a tribute once again to Seurat's intelligence that he was able to assimilate him with so little hesitation or wastage. The moment was critical for him. Since November 1880 he had been back in Paris, living at 19 rue de Chabrol and concerning himself with the question 'What ought a picture to be?' Somehow, and most probably from Sensier's book, he may have found that Millet had studied the Parthenon friezes, from which Seurat had made drawings six years before. Given Seurat's thoroughgoing and ruminative turn of mind it is very unlikely that he did not pursue the subject further. Assuming that he did so, it is again unlikely that he did not realize that Millet had found a way, as Puvis had not, of integrating his feeling for the antique into an interpretation of what was actually going on in the France of his day.

We cannot be sure of the paintings by Millet which Seurat knew at first hand, but it is at least possible that the *Ruth and Boaz* of 1853 suggested to him the uses of the frieze as a method of treating late nineteenth-century country subjects, just as the *Peasant Putting her Bread in the Oven* of 1854 showed how a timeless grandeur could be conferred on the materials of genre-painting. In Seurat's *Dans Un Pré* (*Ill. 42*) the cow may well have been lifted direct from Millet's *Peasant with her Cow* of 1859; Robert L. Herbert has pointed out that Millet's *Twilight* of *c.* 1866, now in the Boston Museum of Fine Arts, looks forward to Seurat's mature style of drawing. One could, in fact, suggest that during the period immediately preceding the preparation of the *Baignade* Seurat was very largely concerned with painting derivatives of Millet's subject-matter—and painting them, what is more, in Millet's own countryside. (As late as October 1883, for instance, he is on record as having stayed at the Auberge Ganne in Barbizon.) Two contrasted themes predominate in Seurat's Barbizon period: the iconography of vigorous action, in which harvester and woodcutter and stone-breaker (*Ills. 38, 39*) whisk us back by way of Millet (see the *Potato-Planters* of 1862) to the fifth and fourth centuries B.C.; and the iconography of immobility: cryptic and monumental studies of seated figures or single haystacks (*Ills. 34, 41*). These were subjects which Millet threw in as part of a full-scale composition, but Seurat abstracted them for his own purposes, as if to see how far he could confer dignity, not to say awe, on individual incidents in country life.

In the little panels of stone-breakers (*Ill. 105*) Seurat took over a theme that had been famous in French painting since 1849, when Courbet painted his enormous (ten feet by seven) study of the subject. After Proudhon had described this in 1864 as the first true socialist picture the subject must have had overtones of social criticism for anyone as intelligent as Seurat; and, as Mr Robert L. Herbert has pointed out, Millet in the 1850s was quick to propose a variant of Courbet's *La Rencontre* in which the social alignments are subtly corrected.

41 *Figure Massive dans un Paysage à Barbizon*, oil on panel, *c*. 1882: despite its modest proportions (6 inches by 9) this is a painting that recalls the hieratic dignity of the Egyptian seated figures that Seurat had studied in the Louvre

42 *Vaches dans un Pré*, oil on panel, *c*. 1883: a companion-piece to *Ill. 36*, and no less remarkable for its purely painterly qualities

But in Seurat's panels there is a frankly experimental note, and the experiment relates more to the excitements of liberated colour than to the social implications of the subject-matter (*Ills. 44, 48*). Delacroix is there, as much as Courbet; fragmented brushwork and freely vibrating colour are what Seurat was primarily interested in, and there are portents of the frieze-like structure, the flattened arrangement of figures along the picture-plane, which was to be a feature of more than one of his later masterpieces. Unlike several of his followers, Seurat was never doctrinaire in his attitude to colour-theory: as Mr Herbert says of the little *Stone Breaker* which was given to Yale in 1959, 'Not only do the combinations of hues fail to fall into place as logically applied theory, but the generous strokes of

43 *Le Chemin Creux*, oil on canvas, *c.* 1882: one of the paintings in which Seurat came nearest to orthodox Barbizonian practice

44 *Paysan au Travail*, oil on panel, 1883: an instance of the care with which Seurat carried over into his early panels the principles he followed also in his drawings—the harmonizing of opposites, for example, and the simplification of the rearground into flat bands or strips of contrasting tone

lavender over the greens, the light orange patch beneath the pile of stones, or here and there the exposed golden-brown of the wood shows us the marks of a very gifted colourist.'

And, no matter what is owed in these early paintings to Millet, to Corot, to Puvis, and to Barbizon in general, they also look forward to the future. Theodore Rousseau may have godfathered early panels like the *Coucher de Soleil* of *c.* 1882 (CdH 8), just as Corot stands behind the *Clairière* of the same period (CdH 21); but when Seurat treats his figures as flat silhouettes brought up parallel to the picture-plane, and when the actions of those figures are reduced to a schema of flailing diagonals, then the point of reference is as much to Malevich's view of agriculture as to Millet's. Seurat excels, moreover, in his ability to combine the most rigorous formal investigations with a paint-structure that is consummately poetical.

45 *Le Jardinier*, oil on panel, *c.* 1882

If Seurat's genius was continually on the move, it was partly because he was entirely unprejudiced in his attitude to the potentialities of the image. He was as interested in the eye-catching simplifications of the popular broadsheet as he was in Egyptian or Assyrian art, and as ready to learn from Flaxman as from the posters of his own day. He read enormously, and much of what he read (the Goncourts, Huysmans, Zola, in particular) related to the problem of how best to get modern life into literature: on what terms, that is to say, it should be admitted. He lived in an age when the idea of scientific exactitude was gaining ground over the idea of romantic impulse; and when he came back from the army in November

1880 he studied especially the theoretical literature of colour, which was at that moment being rapidly enlarged, and the possibility of establishing what might be called a grammar and syntax of visual phenomena. In particular he got hold of the French translation, published in 1881, of Ogden Rood's *Modern Chromatics*, and in later years he was at pains to express how much he owed to it. He also had in his studio an annotated copy of Sutter's *Phenomena of Vision*. The grand object of his studies was, very briefly, to bring to consciousness and formulate impulses, attitudes, patterns of feeling and physical predispositions which had hitherto belonged to the unconscious. In this respect Seurat was trying to do something that would be done in another sphere by the pioneers of psycho-analysis; but, unlike them, he had the benefit of a current of experiment which, after an uncertain start, ran strongly his way.

Seurat was 'not an easy man to know'. In his person he had a distinguished and somewhat rarefied appearance. 'Imagine', wrote Jules Christophe in the year of Seurat's death, 'a tall young fellow,

46 *Vers le Bourg*, oil on panel, *c.* 1883

timid as could be, but with an energy no less extreme than his shyness; the beard of an Apostle and a girlish sweetness of manner; a voice deep, hooded, quick to win others to his point of view; one of those peaceable but immensely obstinate people whom you expect to be frightened of everything and whom, in reality, nothing can deter.' Another friend said that Seurat was 'like Donatello's St George, which is now in the Bargello in Florence', and a third likened his profile to that of 'an Assyrian ruler'. All agreed that, as Gustave Kahn said later, 'Seurat thought out his projects a long way ahead and carried them through to the end'. Seurat had, in fact, precisely the looks and the temperament which went with his ambition; and although he was only thirty-one when he died, many of his friends would have agreed with what Signac wrote in his diary in 1894:

47 *La Charrette Attelée*, oil on canvas, *c.* 1883

48 *Les Terrassiers*, oil on panel, *c.* 1882–3: an anthology, almost, of Seurat's current preoccupations—the foreground divided into zones of criss-crossed colour, the figures glimpsed at a moment of strenuous activity, the cart silhouetted against the sky and a hint, in the up-ended shaft, of something more ominous than the every-day ways of the countryside

'Some critics say that Seurat didn't leave a life's work behind him, but it seems to me that, on the contrary, he gave what he had to give, and gave it admirably. He would certainly have painted many more pictures, and made further headway, but his task was completed. He had passed the painter's problems in review and said the last word, more or less, on all of them: black and white, harmony of line, composition, colour-harmony and colour contrast . . . and even the frame. What more can one ask of a painter?'

Meanwhile, all this remained to be done. Seurat had to settle for himself, and by himself, the problems presented by (i) the science of colour, (ii) the psychological implications of design, (iii) the uses of proportion (or, in Robert Rey's phrase, of 'non-accidental numbers') in large-scale composition. He had also to decide on the subject-matter most appropriate to a genuinely modern art.

49 *Fort de la Halle*, 1882–3: whereas in his early oil-panels of the countryside Seurat was still clearly feeling his way, drawings like this one prove that at that same period he was in full command of an entirely original mode of expression

50 *Les Deux Campagnards,* c. 1883

51 *Le Poulain,* c. 1883

Seurat's approach to these problems was characteristically deliberate. While the question of colour was working itself out in his mind, he forswore colour altogether. His object was, also, to get away from library-art. Library-art and life-room art had between them made up almost his entire output up till the winter of 1879–80. In studying Ingres, Holbein and Raphael Seurat had devoted himself to those 'eternal and immutable' values which Baudelaire, in 1863, had declared to be half of art. Thenceforward he turned to the Baudelairean second half: to modernity, conceived as 'the transitory, the fugitive, the contingent'. Baudelaire went on to say that 'before *modernity* can be worthy to turn into antiquity, the artist must extract from it that mysterious beauty which human life puts into it involuntarily'. *Involuntarily*: that is the keyword. Seurat's aim, here as elsewhere, was to take the involuntary and transform it, by an effort of the organized will, into one of the ingredients of high art.

52 *Attelage près d'Arbres Grêles, c.* 1883

53 *Le Carriole et le Chien, c.* 1883: in drawings like this one, and like *Ill. 52*, Seurat anticipates, surely, some of the great black-and-white images of the silent cinema

54 *Dans la Rue*, Conté crayon, *c*. 1883

CHAPTER TWO

Seurat the Draughtsman

In his drawings, Seurat began with the classic art-student's drudgeries. But he brought to them celestial qualities of his own; and he very soon learned to take a small fragment of everyday life and isolate and simplify it. He had reproductions of drawings by both Millet and Rembrandt in his studio, and before long he perfected the kind of drawing for which he is best known: drawing in which line (in Ingres' sense) plays almost no part and the thick-grained paper is rubbed with a soft, fatty Conté crayon in such a way that the artist has at his disposal a gamut ranging from the most brilliant and velvety blacks to a white that is, as Leibniz would say, 'furiously white'. Robert L. Herbert has this to say of the Michallet paper which Seurat always used: 'it is a thick rag paper, milk-white when fresh but a creamy off-white after exposure to the air. Under a microscope its myriad tufts can be seen to project from the surface in little comma-shaped hooks. When Seurat lightly stroked its surface, the hooks caught the crayon here and there, leaving the valleys between them untouched. As a result, his greys are truly three-dimensional, with the white showing between the touches of dark, and no matter how smooth when viewed from a distance they are full of little wisps and irregularities which are a joy to discover when close to the eye.' 'One of the marvels of such drawings', he goes on to say, 'is in the realisation that this light is actually the white paper showing through between the strokes of crayon. We instinctively think of the artist illuminating the darkness with his light, because we associate it with a natural light source. We tend to imagine him moving it about as though it were the mobile stuff of his art, whereas in fact it is the *dark* which he pushes on to the paper.' Anyone who has handled a mature Seurat drawing will know what Signac meant when he said that 'These are the most beautiful painter's drawings that ever existed. Thanks to Seurat's perfected mastery of values, one can say that his "black-and-whites" are more luminous, and even more full of colour than many a painting in oils.'

As early as *c.* 1881, according to César de Hauke's dating, Seurat was making drawings of the sort, and of the quality, that Signac had in mind: and the drawings dated '*c.* 1882' by M. de Hauke include many single figures that are as beautiful as any in the canon. But the point of the early drawings is not merely how or when he arrived, but what he got up to on the way there. No comprehensive exhibition of his drawings has ever been held: there is a case, therefore, for a rapid run-through of some of the questions which are raised by the drawings, nearly three hundred in number, which pre-date the *Baignade*.

55 *Les Vaches*, Conté crayon, *c.* 1881

56 *Le Glaneur*, Conté crayon, *c.* 1883

57 *Usines sous la Lune, c.* 1883: one of the drawings in which Seurat proved that the reaper and the sower had no monopoly of 'high art' and that the industrial revolution was every bit as worthy of consideration. Many parallels could be found in the naturalistic novels of the day

Already at the age of seven, according to family tradition, Seurat made pencil-drawings which, as I have said, curiously foreshadow his later practice: two of these are illustrated by M. de Hauke. But for most practical purposes the corpus of his drawings begins with his admission at the age of sixteen to the local Ecole Municipale du Dessin. Here he began with the beginner's traditional exercises—drawing from casts, above all—though he did break out in order to draw, for instance, the statue of Vercingetorix (CdH 217) by Aimé Millet, and in one very early drawing (CdH 218) he studied the outline of an architectural detail which traced the capital letter 'S'. At the age of sixteen he made a drawing (CdH 221) from a cast of

58 *Lecture, c.* 1883–4: though infinitely more adventurous in his attitude to society, Seurat was as sensitive as Bonnard or Vuillard to the healing quiet of the home

the reclining figure of Ilissus on the Parthenon frieze, and in a very short while he could draw from the antique with the perfect equanimity and impartiality which was to distinguish so many of his later investigations. Lequien, his first master, was a sculptor who in his youth had come second in the Prix de Rome, and one can sense that he guided Seurat towards an ideal purity and suavity of modelling, and a bland and ivorine texture that aimed rather to counterfeit the surface of marble than to release the capacities inherent in pencil and paper.

When Seurat moved to the Ecole des Beaux-Arts and began to work under Henri Lehmann there was a marked widening in his possibilities. Lehmann was a former student of Ingres, and in the series of drawings from the male nude which form nos. 272 to 282 in de Hauke (*Ills. 10, 11*) Seurat seems to me to have aimed at the kind of heroic neo-classicism, midway between naturalism and the antique, which marks such early subject-paintings as the *Envoys from Agamemnon*, with which Ingres won the first Prix de Rome in 1801;

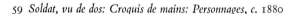

59 *Soldat, vu de dos: Croquis de mains: Personnages, c.* 1880

this is a picture which Seurat could have seen at the Ecole des Beaux-Arts. Seurat was doubtless told, too, of the noble half-length with which Ingres won the so-called '*prix du torse*' in 1802. Seurat's early attempts at the female nude include a copy after a drawing for Ingres' *Antiochus and Stratonice*; and he followed the Ingrist tradition in another early drawing (CdH 255) which is from a reproduction of a drawing by Raphael. Later, when he was drawing and painting as an independent artist, he still kept on occasion to Ingres' practice of filling the paper or the canvas with a group of unrelated subjects: a feature of nearly all the drawings that Seurat did in the army (*Ill. 59*), this recurs also in paintings like the *Dans la Rue* of *c.* 1883 (*Ill. 60*). Seurat also did a painting (CdH 1) and a drawing (CdH 315) after the figure of Angelica in Ingres' *Angélique au Rocher*; and when at a much later stage in his life he planned his *Poseuses* (*Ill. 187*) it is difficult to believe that he did not have somewhere in his mind, for the left-hand figure, the *Baigneuse de Valpinçon* of Ingres. Ingres' practice had been held up to him as something near the ideal; and having himself copied

60 *Dans la Rue*, oil on panel, *c.* 1883

61 (*left*) *Frileuse, Tête de Profil, c.* 1877: an early Ingrist drawing

62 *Le Berger Endormi, c.* 1878: conceivably something is owed to Corot in the tenderness of the landscape in this student-composition

63 *La Jambe*, 1883–4. A preliminary drawing for the seated boy on the left in the *Baignade* (*Ill. 127*)

anatomical details from Ingres' great symphonic ventures he clearly found it the most natural thing in the world to build up *Une Baignade, Asnières* in part from figure-drawings (concentrated, sometimes, on a single limb, *Ill. 63*) done in the studio. Mr William Homer suggests very plausibly that Seurat may have been influenced at this time by the following passage from Rood's *Modern Chromatics*: 'The advance from drawing to painting should be gradual, and no serious attempts in colour should be made until the student has attained undoubted proficiency in outline and in light and shade. Amateurs universally abandon black and white for colour at a very early stage, and this circumstance alone precludes all chance of progress. . . . If the artist cannot draw objects in full light and shade in a rather masterly way there is no point in his attempting colour.'

Ingres was not, however, the only master who was put in Seurat's way at the Ecole des Beaux-Arts. Holbein was one of many to whom he went in search of one or another of his grounds for confidence; and when he came to make a tentative shot at a composition of figures Puvis and Corot were there to prompt him: Puvis in

64 A page from the Brest notebook of 1880 in which there appears for the first time, in the seated figure on the left, one of the dominant themes of the *Baignade*

the frieze-like disposition of figures (CdH 261–2) and Corot, surely, in the relations of figures to simplified classical landscape in the Louvre's *Berger Endormi* (*Ill. 62*). In the case of some artists it might be pointless to hunt down single sheets whose relevance to later achievement is not always obvious: but with Seurat there is no such thing as an irrelevant piece of evidence. Even if he had not himself made it clear to Fénéon, we should know that everything counted.

Seurat told Fénéon, for instance, that from 1876 onwards he was preoccupied with the problem of colour, and specifically that while in the army at Brest in the first months of 1880 he was thinking over Rood's ideas on the subject. But as far as we know he never touched a paint-brush during that time, confining himself to the small sheets of notebook paper on which he noted down unrelated images with a lead pencil. Most of these were taken from everyday garrison life, with an occasional café-table, or a provincial shoe-

74

maker (*Ill. 65*), or a horse and cart, to vary the repertory. Seurat put off all his art-school airs, in these rapid sketches, and tried for a brisk vernacular notation that would get the sense of the subject down on paper as quickly as possible. One could turn page after page and suppose that he had put all grander designs out of mind 'for the duration'. But this would be a great mistake. For suddenly, on one corner of a piece of paper measuring six inches by nine and a half (*Ill. 64*), there turns up not merely a first draft for the seated boy on the left of *Une Baignade, Asnières*, but a draft also for Seurat's treatment of the grass beneath and behind him. Meditating on Rood's theories, he must have seen them borne out by someone who had sat down for a moment in the sun. Quick to note it down, he harboured the idea throughout the rest of his time in the army; and eventually, after more than one attempt at painting seated figures on sloping grassland (*Ills. 110, 111*), he was able to work it up into one of the grandest of all European paintings.

65 *Un Cordonnier, c.* 1879–80: one of the earliest and most elegant of Seurat's studies of everyday life

66 *Le Clown Rouge, c.* 1880: an early instance of Seurat's preoccupation with the circus, which was to be the subject of his last major figure-composition

67 *Banquistes, c.* 1880: a foretaste, again, of preoccupations which later resulted in the great *Parade de Cirque*

68 *Danseuse de Corvi, c.* 1880

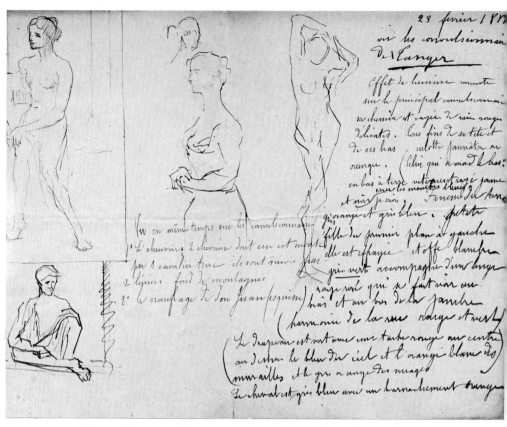

69 A sheet of notes made in February 1881 from Delacroix's *Convulsionnaires de Tanger*, at a time when Seurat had not yet begun to paint regularly in oils

This is one of the things for which it is worth while to search through Seurat's early drawings. It cannot, equally, be accidental that when Seurat was back in Paris and living in the rue de Chabrol (a street which runs into the Boulevard de Magenta) he made five drawings which look forward to two masterpieces of his last years: *La Parade* and *Le Cirque*. One of these (CdH 382) is of the entrance to the Cirque Corvi; alone among Seurat's early drawings, it bears specific colour-notations. Another, *Ill. 67*, is a first shot, as is also *Ill. 68*, at the iconography of performance: in the handling of the dancer, half goddess, half captive animal, there is already the sympathetic understanding which makes Seurat, for all his impassivity,

70 *A Demi Couchée, c.* 1881: like a news-photographer, Seurat aimed to get in close to the subject, even if part of it turned out to be cut off by his angle of vision

no less moving than Daumier when he sets himself to portray those who live by pleasing others. There is a first sight, too, of the circus ring and the clown (*Ill. 66*). And in February 1881, while Seurat's colour-practice in his paintings was still hesitant and unformed, there are elaborate handwritten colour-notes on a sheet of drawings from Delacroix's *Convulsionnaires de Tanger* (*Ill. 69*).

Not long after Seurat's return to Paris he began to draw in quite a different way, with long diagonal strokes through which the forms seem, as it were, to push their way upwards towards the spectator. This technique he applied to a long series of single figures (*Ills. 71–3*), many of which he brought forward until they filled the

71 (*left*) *Assise, les Mains Croisées, c.* 1881

72 (*right*) *Reparant son Manteau, c.* 1880–1

picture-space and not seldom burst out of it at the top. Gradually, as we study these drawings, the vigorous cross-hatching gives way to a more mysterious, less abruptly accented procedure, until in the end we have something very near to the perfection of Seurat's mature style. The drawing modulates from the deepest, most velvety blacks right through to the natural white of the paper; no longer are we conscious of individual pencil-strokes, but merely of a process of

73 *Couseuse, un Tableau au Mur*, Conté crayon, c. 1881

74 *Cireur de Bottes et son Client*, c. 1881. Robert L. Herbert points out that this drawing is related to 'the shadow-plays popular in the 1880s'

uninterrupted *becoming*. From a drawing like *Couseuse, Un Tableau au Mur* (*Ill. 73*), which Degas or even Whistler could appropriate without incongruity, we come suddenly upon the *Cireur de Bottes et son Client* (*Ill. 74*), which is like nothing else in art: that nervous economical outline, those luxurious blacks and the meaningful opposition of that palest white could only be signed 'Seurat'. These are the drawings which poets and fellow-artists have always coveted: from Paul Valéry to Paul Eluard, and from Bonnard and Vuillard

75 *Groupe de Gens devant une Usine, c.* 1883: one of the most mysterious of Seurat's drawings, and one in which the cloaked and hooded figures could well be strike-leaders, anarchists, or saboteurs

to Morandi and Henry Moore, the list is long, and would be longer still if such sheets were not now among the most expensive of French nineteenth-century drawings.

Seurat was, therefore, a mature artist, and in his drawings the master of a fully developed and entirely original style, before he had painted a single picture that could be called his own. This is to overstate hardly at all the situation as it was towards the end of 1881; and thereafter the fascination of his drawings is twofold. Marvellous in themselves, they reveal over and over again the subjects which Seurat had in mind to handle in oils. When he gave Paris a rest, for instance, and went into the country he suddenly

76 *Suivant le Sentier*, Conté crayon, *c.* 1883

77 *Maisons (Effet de Soleil—Paysage aux Maisons) c.* 1881. A landscape-drawing that relates directly to the early oil-panels

brought off a drawing like the *Maisons (Effet de Soleil—Paysage aux Maisons)*, *Ill.* 77, with a decision and an authority that he was still a long way from acquiring at the easel. Sometimes, as in the Museum of Modern Art's *Casseur de Pierres et autres Personnages, Le Raincy (Ill.* 78), he would return from a visit to his father in the suburbs with a drawing that was like an anthology of the motifs he wanted one day to paint: the odd rhomboid shapes of wall and roof, the contrast of white shirt and dark trousers in the figure of the stone-breaker, and the ordered construction of each individual plane within the picture.

Just occasionally a drawing would come, almost entire, from one of Seurat's heroes: Millet, for instance, in the *Crépuscule (Ill.* 79). But

these are rarities: it is more usual for Seurat to probe the bent work-
man, the silhouetted horse, and the mysterious stranger in the
metropolitan twilight, in terms that are all his own. As happened
with the boy on the grass at Brest, there are cases in which a key-
element in Seurat's later imagery stalks in unannounced: above all,
perhaps, the nursemaid, first seen in drawings of *c.* 1882 (*Ills. 130,
142*), who turns up on the grass in the *Grande Jatte* with the tone-
relations of her cap and cloak reversed.

   Drawing did of course remain an independent activity throughout
Seurat's career, and it could be argued that some of the greatest of
his late works are to be found among the drawings. But since many

78 *Casseur de Pierres et autres Personnages, Le Raincy, c.* 1881. One of the most complex of Seurat's early pencil-studies of the industrial suburbs

79 *Crépuscule du Soir, c.* 1885: a drawing directly related to J.-F. Millet

80 *La Route de la Gare*, Conté crayon, *c.* 1882

drawings did, in the event, lead to great paintings, it is only human to regret that certain themes were not taken further in this way. Among the unpainted masterworks to which Seurat might have devoted his gifts had he lived longer are, surely, the railway-subject which is adumbrated in several drawings of *c.* 1882 (*Ills. 80–82*); the human drama of *la zone*, that grim region on the outskirts of Paris which is neither town nor country (*Ills. 85, 86*); the great formal Parisian landscapes which are hinted at, in the drawings of the Place de la Concorde (*Ills. 83, 84*), in terms which look forward seventy years to Giacometti; and, among subjects from everyday life, the large-scale building-site, as to which one or two tantalizing notes were made (*Ills. 87, 89*).

90

81 (*above*) *La Voie Ferrée, c.* 1182.   82 (*below*) *Locomotive, c.* 1882

83 *Place de la Concorde, l'Hiver, c.* 1883

84 *Place de la Concorde, c.* 1883

85 *La Zone, c.* 1883

86 *Le Chiffonier, c.* 1883

87 *L'Échafaudage, c.* 1883

88 (*below*) *Le Fiacre, c.* 1885: a drawing which, like *Ill. 90,* looks forward to Bonnard's deft and witty explorations of the Parisian street

89 *Le Couvieur, c.* 1883

90 *(below) Rencontre, c.* 1883

95

91 *Le Soir Familial*, *c*. 1883: a subject, again, that was to be a favourite with the Nabis

One can imagine Seurat going forward from *Le Cirque* to tackle these subjects one after another in his paintings, with ever-greater organizational powers and that quality of serene omnicompetence which would surely have made him the greatest picture-architect of the twentieth century. Nor is this to overlook the drawings in which he roughed out themes which were to occupy others for the next quarter of a century: the classic intimist subject, for instance, in *Soir Familial* (*Ill. 91*), and the Vuillard-like *Devant le Balcon* (*Ill. 92*). And, finally, there are the crayon-portraits of his mother and father (*Ills. 8, 9, 93*), of Paul Signac, and of Aman-Jean (*Ill. 22*).

92 *Devant le Balcon, c.* 1883–4

93 *Le Dineur, c.* 1883–4: a famous drawing of Seurat's father at table

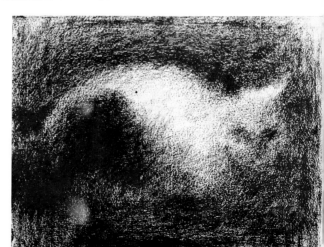

94 *Le Chat, c.* 1883

95 *Par la Grille du Balcon, c.* 1883–4: Vuillard, in his apartment in Place Vintimille, was to treat a similar subject over and over again

96 *Troncs d'Arbres Reflétés dans l'Eau, c.* 1883

One can only regret that it was left to Signac (admirable as his painting is) to make a full-scale portrait of Fénéon, and that Seurat painted only one identifiable human subject: the likeness of his mistress Madeleine Knobloch (*Ill. 209*), which is now in the Courtauld Gallery in London.

There are also drawings even at this relatively early stage in which Seurat went further than he ever learned, or perhaps cared, to go in oils. An instance of this is the drawing of tree-trunks reflected in water (*Ill. 96*): the motif is a favourite with Seurat, but in this case the autonomous beauty of the instrument he had created seems to take over from nature and it is the majesty of the thing brought into being, not of the thing evoked, that captures our attention. But this

97 *Deux Hommes Marchant dans un Champ*, c. 1883

98 *Le Cocher de Fiacre, c.* 1882

rarely occurred: what was more common, at this stage, was for Seurat to take a subject which already embodied the contrasts of black and white which were inherent in his new manner of drawing. This he did, for instance, in the *Cocher de Fiacre (Ill. 98)*, where the coachwork and the coachman's hat offer the desired counterpoise to black, and in the *Deux Hommes Marchant dans un Champs (Ill. 97)* where the white trousers of the nearer man fulfil the same function. Not until much later was he able to keep a perfect balance between the intimations of nature and the demands of a subtle but particularly imperious style.

99 *L'Homme à la Houe*, c. 1883

By the time he was twenty-three, therefore, Seurat had evolved in his drawing what was, in effect, a new instrument of artistic expression. In oils he was at a comparatively tentative stage in his development, but the small paintings which precede the sketches for the *Baignade* are remarkable both for themselves and for what they portend. Nearly all were made in the open air, directly *sur le motif*. Most are on small pieces of board, often no more than six inches by nine, and they show that Seurat took some time to lighten his palette, and longer still to make his first experiments in the vision of colour. His mastery of drawing led him, at first, to balance his masses, light against dark, in a way derived from crayon-drawing; but before long he was producing paintings which are entirely his own—and were conceived, what is more, in terms of oil paint alone.

100 *Maison sous les Arbres,* *c.* 1883: sometimes called *The Haunted House*, this is one of the very few drawings by Seurat in which nature is allowed to verge on the conventionally picturesque

101 *Sous-bois à Pontaubert*, c. 1883–7. Mr Homer has pointed out that: 'The underpainting is composed of sombre earth colours, which Seurat did not use after 1884; but subsequent layers of pigment were applied in a pointillist manner characteristic of 1886–7.' But the basic impulse in this beautiful picture can be dated to the outset of Seurat's career in oils

102 *Banlieue sous la neige*, oil on panel, *c.* 1883

The Clark *Sous-bois*, for instance (*Ill. 101*), was painted at Pontaubert (Yonne). It is Barbizonian in the drenched green foliage, and it
owes something to Corot in the delicate alignment of branches and
trunks; but it also reveals, for the first time in oils, Seurat's extraordinary gift for the maintenance throughout the picture of a
perfectly unemphatic handling. He may have quoted to Félix
Fénéon Corot's remark about the '*point lumineux . . . qui doit être
unique*', but in this early canvas he keeps to an absolute regularity of
touch. Others of his Barbizonian pictures have the authentic,
browny, vespertinal look: Seurat is more himself in the informal
suburban landscapes and townscapes in which, with earth colours
and a regular criss-cross stroke, he took the world head-on, chose a
small fragment from the view that presented itself, disposed of it on
his canvas in clearly marked zones of interest, cut out a terrace of
horizontals in the space before him, and made as much as he could of
the silhouettes, right angles and diagonals that architecture offered

(*Ills. 102, 103*). Horizontals he could always find in nature: for the verticals which complemented them he sought out subjects whose verticals were ready-made by human agency. These procedures are shown to perfection in factory subjects like the Lévy *Banlieue* of 1882 (*Ill. 109*), which was to be taken up by Van Gogh in 1887, and in the series of paintings of peasants knocking stakes into the ground. Seurat also at this time made the studies of peasants reaping, scything (*Ills. 105, 106*) and breaking stones which relate closely to Millet, though with the difference that Seurat was at least as interested in flattening and simplifying his forms, or in balancing the white of a shirt against the dark of a pair of trousers, as he was in the ardours and virtues of labour.

This period can also show some paintings of a more purely enigmatic character. Much as Kandinsky, for instance, dragged an onion-top church tower into his *Improvisation, 1912*, so Seurat made use of certain recurrent forms in a way which, while never wresting

103 *Ruines des Tuileries*, oil on panel, *c.* 1882

104 (*above*) *Maisons dans les Arbres*, oil on panel, *c.* 1883

105 (*above right*) *Casseur de Pierres à la Brouette, Le Raincy*, oil on panel, *c.* 1883

106 (*right*) *Le Faucheur*, oil on panel, *c.* 1883

107 (*above*) *Paysan à la Houe*, oil on canvas, *c.* 1883

them from their immediate identity, none the less suggests that they
have a universal validity quite irrespective of the connotation which
they bear at the moment. An instance of this is the *Meule de Foin* of
c. 1883 (*Ill. 34*) in which the stack has an outline identical with that
of the old woman who sits with her back to us in the *Grande Jatte*.
Equally curious is the *Figure Massive dans un Paysage* (*Ill. 41*)
in which the brooding, priest-like silhouette sits as massively in its
skirts as does a seated Egyptian scribe on its base of stone. Were the
perspective exact, this figure would be well over life-size; and equally

110

108 (*right*) *La Vespasienne*, oil on panel, *c.* 1882

109 *Banlieue*, oil on panel, *c.* 1882–3: an early example of Seurat's attempts to paint the industrial suburbs in accordance with the principles of divisionism

in the Glasgow single figure of a boy sitting in the grass (*Ill. 111*), where the subject is seen, from above and close to, against a rearground of strong sunlight, there is an element of the colossal which has no equivalent in the *pleinairiste* paintings of Pissarro from which Seurat took his general scheme. We see, in short, that already in his first two years as an independent painter Seurat was beginning to deny conventional perspective and conventional space: this tendency was to reach its climax in the *Grande Jatte*.

110 *Paysanne assise dans l'Herbe*, oil on canvas, *c.* 1882

111 *Petit Paysan assis dans un Pré*, oil on canvas, *c.* 1882

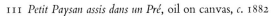

112 *Nu Assis*, a drawing in Conté crayon of 1883–4, is a study for the figure who appears just right of centre in the finished *Baignade*

CHAPTER THREE

The First of the Great Pictures

In physical terms, there is no mystery at all about the evolution of *Une Baignade, Asnières*. Few great pictures are so well documented in all their stages. From the moment that the riverside, as a source of subjects, enters Seurat's *œuvre* with the *Personnages dans un Pré* (CdH 41), the *Pêcheur à la Ligne* (CdH 64) and the *Bateaux près de la Berge, Asnières* (CdH 76) right through the long series of direct sketches to the final study (*Ill. 124*) and the painting itself (*Ill. 127*), the history of the *Baignade* is readily traced.

From the fourteen painted panels and the ten drawings which relate directly to the *Baignade* (I exclude, here, a number of works in both media which have an indirect relationship with the great canvas), we can see what Seurat took from nature, what he worked up or perfected for himself in the studio, and what he considered taking from nature but finally left out. In this last category come a number of motifs which were dear to him in other contexts: the black and the white horses, for instance, which appear in *Ills. 117, 118* and *121*; the silhouetted man in dark clothing and bowler hat, from *Ill. 123*; and the long flat form of the moored boat in *Ill. 116*. Among the things that he seems to have got up for himself are the dog, and its relation to the back of the reclining man beside him (*Ills. 125, 127*); the hallooing boy to the extreme right, as to whom Sir Kenneth Clark says that 'I have a feeling that one day I shall find his prototype in antique painting'; and—curious detail—the sharp curving edge of the sail silhouetted against the trees of the Grande Jatte. This is a form that does not occur in any of the oil-sketches for the *Baignade*, and I suspect that it had a ritual significance for Seurat, and accorded with the theories of meaningful line to which he adhered, and which I shall discuss later.

In general, the five main figures and the still-life of clothes in the *Baignade* all owe more to the studio than to the observations which

113 *Homme Peignant son Bateau*, oil on panel, *c.* 1883

Seurat made on the spot. More exactly: they were prompted, beyond a doubt, by the free-and-easy life of the foreshore; but when Seurat began to build up his final composition he felt the need to do them all over again from the naked model in his studio. And this is what he did, making a particularly careful job of the reclining man in the foreground to the left and a marvellously poetical and

Piero-esque one of the boy just right of centre (*Ill. 112*). Where life, as revealed in the sketches, was chaotic and unbiddable, Seurat introduced an element of total serenity in which the thing seen and the thing imagined become as one.

The *Baignade* oil sketches were done sometimes in the criss-cross technique of certain independent panels (*Ill. 113*), but more often in pure Impressionist style, with long flat lozenges of pure colour and a good deal of brisk shorthand in the drawing. To anyone who studies these sketches and has tried to find the point on the bank of the Seine from which Seurat viewed his subject, it will be evident that in the final version he departed considerably from the *données* of nature. So far, for instance, from presenting, as it does in the picture, the aspect of an unimpeded vast, this arm of the river is narrow and constricted. And although the factories may well not have had their present blackened, gap-toothed and elderly appearance, the sketches would indicate that they must have been altogether more lively and varied in colour, and less suave and coherent in design, than the *Baignade* suggests (*Ill. 114*).

As far as colour was concerned, Seurat was already working on the divisionist technique, and in 1887 he went over the finished picture again and added a number of pure divisionist passages; but neither in the sketches nor in the pictures as first shown does he attempt a thoroughgoing divisionist style: this was surely because he had not completed his grasp of it, and not, as Signac suggested, because he felt bound to make certain concessions to public taste.

Instructive as it is to follow the *Baignade* through its many re-organizations, it is the finished picture that has most to tell us about Seurat. It is, to begin with, a prodigious feat. The final sketch is less than one-twelfth the size of the *Baignade*, and there is no indication, there or elsewhere, of the multiple techniques which Seurat was to employ in the picture itself (*Ill. 127*). No one could have foreseen, for instance, the Leonardesque value-contrasts with which the central figure is given a final monumentality; or the fact that Seurat would half undress the seated boy on the left in order to relate him rather to the grassy bank than to the contrasted blacks and whites of the fore-ground figures; or that the smaller of the two figures in the water would come up immediately athwart the patch of reeds. (Perhaps Seurat himself did not foresee this, since the figure seems to have been painted over the reeds, whereas in the final sketch he comes well below them.)

If we had no sketches at all for the *Baignade*, we might imagine that this most ruminative of painters had bodied the picture forth in one great thrust of the imagination, drawing for the purpose upon the existing repertory of his themes and so combining them that naturalistic beginnings were carried over into a vast architectural scheme. We would point, first, to the schema of verticals and horizontals, as telling as anything in geometrical abstract painting, which Seurat devised for the bridge and the grouped factories beyond. Next would come the landscape in the left middleground, where the foliage has the all-purpose fuzz of the *Ville d'Avray, Maisons Blanches* (*Ill. 40*) and the walls and building-faces have precisely the rectangular forms and space-regulating function which Seurat assigned to them in many earlier pictures. We might see in the treatment of the grass Seurat's most extended attempt to date at the divisionist handling of local colour; and we might also think that the Seine itself is still handled in a modified Impressionist style. (Both Renoir and Monet had painted this reach of the river.) We would certainly note that the modelling of the naked backs was in perfectly orthodox style, with no forecast of the divisionist treatment of flesh that Seurat was to employ four years later in *Les Poseuses*. Technically, altogether, we should rank this as a transitional picture, and we might wonder if the passage of time has not tended to obscure its inconsistencies of style by producing a general flattening of colour-contrasts.

Seurat had studied, among other things, the colour-circle devised by Rood from which the complementary of each colour could be seen at a glance: purple/green, blue/yellow-orange, yellow/ultramarine, violet/greeny yellow, and so forth. Already in the *Baignade* there are spasmodic attempts to put this into practice; but even in the later *Grande Jatte* Seurat's first and greatest elucidator, Félix Fénéon, was able to point to passages in which the principle was not carried through. Fénéon was doubly handicapped, in any case, in his attempts to explain the procedure. For one thing, Seurat was morbidly secretive: 'I'd have liked Fénéon to go direct to Seurat and ask him,' Pissarro wrote to his son, 'but that's out of the question.' For another, the concept of scientific purity presented great chemical difficulties: here Fénéon's evidence is once again invaluable, in that it shows us how the problem looked at the time when it was being tackled. Light and time were harmful to certain colours; others

114 *Les Deux Rives*, oil on panel, *c.* 1883. The final version of the *Baignade* is, of course, a minutely constructed rearrangement of the scene as it actually presented itself to Seurat. This early and unpopulated oil-sketch is certainly nearer to 'reality'

fought with their neighbours to their mutual disadvantage; 'silver-white, which has a lead base, goes black, and zinc-white, which does not go black, is too thin . . .' Not for nothing did Fénéon remark that 'the painter who took most care with the manufacture of his colours is precisely the one whose colours have blackened most: Leonardo.'

But nowhere, among all these convolutions of subject, vision, chemistry and technique, can we detach the secret of the *Baignade's* extraordinary and secret appeal. Anyone who has been to Arezzo will recognize, to begin with, that after the 1860s and 1870s, when the masterpieces of the day were painted from a radiant but funda-mentally mindless view of the world, an artist has reached back into the past and struck one of the great bell-notes of human com-munication. Seurat has produced order from chaos, the eternal from the fugitive, and ideal proportion from a scene which, in life, would have tugged all ways at once. Many people take Piero della Francesca

115 *Cinq Figures d'Hommes*, oil on panel, *c.* 1883: like *Ill. 116* on the next page, this little sketch is a draft, made *sur le motif*, of elements which might or might not find a place in the final picture

116 *La Seine*, oil on panel, *c.* 1883

to be the source of this, and copies of two of his frescoes can be found to this day in the chapel of the Ecole des Beaux-Arts. But this would not explain why we also feel the *Baignade* to be a profound comment upon modern industrial society.

This is a difficult subject. Seurat's extreme discretion in both writing and speech makes it impossible to say, from first-hand evidence, what his political feelings were. But his closest friends, both in art and in literature, were almost without exception men of the left, with an inclination towards anarchical communism. Dangerous as it is to infer a painter's opinions from his subject-matter (Millet, for instance, was very angry indeed when people assumed that he must be a socialist), I think we may assume that if Seurat had not shared some of his friends' opinions he would certainly have said so, and that some record of his demurral would have come down to us.

When painting the *Baignade* he had not yet met the friends in question; but at that time the mere fact of his wishing to democratize Arcadia and picture it in the likeness of the freshwater pleasures of the working-class was a gesture of defiance. Some scholars have found a kinship between the *Baignade* and Puvis de Chavannes' *Doux Pays* (*Ill. 23*), which Seurat could have seen in 1882, and there are certainly compositional resemblances between the two canvases, as well as a shared yearning for a lost world of harmony and equilibrium and, as I said earlier, a certain kinship of detail. But the point is that Seurat set out to wrest the lost world of harmony and equilibrium from the everyday facts of life in an industrial suburb, whereas Puvis in his daydreams kept *le moderne* at arm's length.

The *Baignade* is not a 'problem picture' like the *Grande Jatte*: but Seurat was already at the stage in his career at which nothing was accidental, and I suspect that the subject-matter of the painting was planned as carefully as its mathematics, or as the relation between the top of the head of the central figure and the roofline of the Clichy factories. It would not for instance surprise me if there were more

117 *Cheval Blanc dans l'Eau*, oil on panel, *c.* 1883. The horse's head, here, is a *revenant* from earlier, unrelated oil-panels; and the uncharacterized factories in the reargroud contrast with *Ill. 118*, where the industrial detail is almost as precise as it is in the finished picture

118 *Personnages Assis et Étendus, Cheval Noir*, oil on panel, *c.* 1883. The seated boy on the left of this sketch has something of his eventual monumentality in the *Baignade*

than meets the eye in a feature of the *Baignade* which he added after the final sketch: the ferry-boat, that is to say, which is being rowed gondola-wise towards the Ile de la Grande Jatte. In the stern of this stands a French national flag, seven or eight feet high, and furled (unruffled, at any rate, by the winds which, from one quarter or another, are playing on the sailboats and the smoke from the factory chimneys). Seated in the boat are a man and a woman; their backs are turned upon the painter and his subjects, and their dark dress and stiff bearing contrast with the bathers' free and easy dishevelment. Is it impossible that this should have been, in Seurat's mind, the bark of officialdom, indifferent if not actually hostile to the unorganized working-men on the bank? A long shot, admittedly: but one not quite illogical, if we remember that the island to which the ferry is making is the Grande Jatte itself—the pleasure-ground, just then being infiltrated by high fashion, which was to be the subject of Seurat's next major canvas.

119 *Homme Portant un Chapeau de Paille, Assis sur l'Herbe*. This very beautiful drawing is a complete work of art in its own right but, as Mr Herbert points out, certain of its features—the irradiation, for instance, peculiar to black-and-white—are carried over into the final painting

It was in the summer of 1884 that Seurat met the man who was to be his most faithful and persistent champion: Paul Signac. Signac was twenty-one years old: it would hardly be too much to say that the whole of his adult life, which continued until 1935, was dominated first by the example and later by the memory of Georges Seurat. Seurat was too much on top of himself, and too much in control of his development, to be swayed by his friends in the way that a very young painter can usually be. But in Signac he found someone who was not only suggestible, but a born propagandist. Signac had an expansive, outgoing nature, and once he had got hold of an idea he could hardly bear not to share it with others. Seurat found this a mixed blessing, in that the ideas in question were usually simplified, if not actually brutalized, in the process of transference; but Signac's enthusiasm had the effect of bringing into general discussion ideas which, given Seurat's hermetic temperament, might otherwise have remained private.

Unlike Seurat and Seurat's earlier friends, Signac owed all his allegiances, at the time of their first meeting, to the Impressionists. As a boy of seventeen he had taken fire from the Monet exhibition at the 'Vie Moderne' and had at once begun to paint in the open air by the Seine. In the first onrush of his enthusiasm he wrote to Monet and said that, living as he did in a milieu that was hostile to Impressionism, and knowing no Impressionist who could give him the right advice, he would very much value the opportunity of paying a call on Monet.

120 *Homme Couché, c.* 1883: a drawing not, in the end, taken up in the finished picture

121 *Cheval Blanc et Cheval Noir dans l'Eau*, c. 1883–4. In this little oil sketch the water is still the main subject of the picture and the horses (later discarded) reach their point of maximum importance

Whether or not Monet responded to this appeal, it is certain that his influence, and that of Sisley, can be found in Signac's early landscapes. Signac had the beginnings of a powerful personality as a painter, and it is possible that his *Nature Morte, Livres et Violettes* of 1883 influenced Van Gogh. By the time he met Seurat he was already a friend of Pissarro and of Guillaumin; and although there is no reason to think that he 'influenced' the development of Seurat's style there were points at which their early careers ran parallel.

Signac was, for instance, one of the first painters to see the point of the industrial suburbs of Paris as a motif: a painting like his *Faubourg de Paris* of 1883 in the Kryl collection, New York, is very near in its subject-matter to Seurat's *Banlieue*, 1883 (*Ill. 109*), even though Signac opted for the lofty skies and far distances of Impressionist tradition, whereas Seurat picked on a handful of details as if with a telescopic lens, and brought them close to the observer. Signac was the first, also, to choose Port-en-Bessin (in 1882) as a summer resort: his enthusiasm persuaded Seurat to go there six years later.

It is conceivable, finally, that Signac's passion for boating, and the fact that he worked in and from his grandfather's house at Asnières, may have encouraged Seurat to concentrate on life as it presented itself in that quarter.

But when all this is said, it is little enough beside the overriding ascendancy which Seurat was quick to gain over his new friend. Of that ascendancy, Signac's classic *D'Eugène Delacroix au Néo-Impressionisme* of 1899 is our most solid reminder: but it can be seen as vividly in the changes which came over Signac's own paintings from the time he met Seurat; and as Signac was never one to keep silent about his opinions we can assume that he talked freely and often about his new friend.

Signac was, of course, by no means the only person to seek Seurat's acquaintance in the summer of 1884; from the moment that *Une Baignade, Asnières* was put on show, Seurat's career was transformed. Not that outwardly it made much difference—so far was Seurat from being distracted that on Ascension Day 1884 he began work on an even larger and more complex venture, the *Grande Jatte*—but

122 *La Seine et Baigneur Nu assis sur la Berge, c.* 1883–4. Again a very small oil-panel, but one of capital importance. For the first time, Seurat got two of the dominant figures for the finished picture into an approximate relationship: the factories in the background also assume something close to their definitive role

his activity had become a matter of concern and controversy to people far beyond his own small circle. This being so, he was often called upon to talk about what he was doing. Not garrulous by nature, he at first did so only when provoked by mis-statement or wooed by some particularly delicate expression of sympathy. The Belgian poet Verhaeren described how Seurat would discuss his work 'calmly, with careful gestures, while his eye never left one and the slow level voice searched for the slightly professional phrase...' 'If I had to describe him in one word,' Verhaeren went on, 'I would say that he was above all an organizer, in the artistic sense of the word. Hazard, luck, chance, the sensation of being carried away—these things meant nothing to him. Not only did he never start painting without knowing where he was going, but his pre-occupation with his pictures went far beyond their success as in-dividual works. They had no real meaning, in his view, unless they proved a certain rule, a certain artistic truth, or marked a conquest of the unknown. If I understood him correctly, I think that he had set himself to pull art clear of the hesitations of vagueness, indecision, and imprecision. Perhaps he thought that the positive and scientific spirit of the day called for a clearer and more substantial method of conquering beauty.'

Verhaeren evoked the 'modesty, the timidity almost' with which Seurat spoke of his activity. But he could not bear to see that activity slighted or misread. Félix Fénéon had venerated Seurat ever since he first saw the *Baignade*, but a loose statement in one of his essays caused Seurat, in June 1890, to make one of his rare and valuable written statements. 'The purity of the element of the spectrum', he wrote, 'is the keystone of technique. Since I first held a brush, I had been looking, with this basis in mind, for a formula of optical painting (1876–84). I had read Charles Blanc at college.'

The importance of this statement lies in the fact that it back-dates to Seurat's seventeenth year a preoccupation which did not come

123 *L'Homme Assis*, 1883–4. Seurat dropped, in the end, the idea of having a fully dressed figure—doubtless because the dark clothing would have interfered with the picture's tonal scheme—but this remains one of the grandest of the preliminary sketches

124 Final sketch for the *Baignade*, 1883–4. Subtle but radical changes were to come —changes of costume, location, emphasis and tonality—and features like the ferry-boat were to make a last-minute appearance. But in essentials, and on a scale less than one-twelfth that of the final picture, this is the *Baignade* itself

clearly into the open till 1882 or 1883. Charles Blanc's *Grammaire des Arts du Dessin* was completed in 1860, and at the time of Seurat's studentship its author was an important figure in the French official art-world. It was, as Blanc said, a work of instruction, and aimed at those who were pursuing humane studies and wished, 'when on the threshold of life, to learn something of that life in its peaceful and poetical aspect'. A book of well over seven hundred large pages, it is at once a history, a manual of established technical practice, and a discreet manifesto. Seurat took a great deal from it: anyone who, for instance, has puzzled over the curious and oriental features of the spectator *Le Cirque* (*Ill. 225*) will find, on Blanc's page 117, those same features reproduced by way of proof that the *physionomie riante* of Chinese architecture is related to the basic Chinese physiognomy and, therefore, to a universal prototype of hilarity. When Blanc argues that the imitation of nature can no longer be considered to be

125 In this Conté crayon drawing of a man lying down, and in the companion drawing, *Ill. 126*, Seurat used studio-models to work up the subject

the aim of art, and that 'so far from art revolving round nature, it is nature that revolves round art, as the earth round the sun', we see foreshadowed Seurat's belief in the selective, controlling, dominating and regulatory powers of the painter. And it is from Blanc, finally, that he may well have had his first glimpse of divisionist theory; for Blanc, following close after Goethe, Delacroix and Chevreul, had noted that 'wherever there are light and shade the shadow will be coloured, however lightly, with the colour complementary to that of the light'.

Seurat's exceptional pertinacity is shown in the fact that, although he must have begun at once to ponder the significance of Blanc's book, he betrayed his objective not at all while he was evolving the manner of drawing that was peculiar to himself. Even in the *Baignade*, as we have seen, he gave it only a limited expression. But from May 1884 onwards he cannot have doubted that, so far from being a solitary seeker after the truths elsewhere not so much as glimpsed, he had with him a select body of *avant-garde* opinion. And within a year or two that opinion was making itself heard.

If no one can tell quite how Seurat regarded all this, it is because he never seems to have doubted that he was right. In his letter to Fénéon he said that on Ascension Day 1884, with the *Baignade* hardly out of his studio, he began '*Grande Jatte, les études et le* tableau': 'the Grande Jatte, the studies and the *picture*'. Also, that the picture was ready for exhibition by March 1885. It does not seem plausible on

126 As with *Ill. 125*, Seurat was using his already perfected technique as a draughts-man to explore the possibilities of contrast between a white-clad torso and a hard black hat. But in the *Baignade* itself, this contrast was lessened at the base of the neck, and heightened lower down by the introduction of a dog in silhouette

127 The final picture: *Une Baignade, Asnières*, painted between 1883 and 1884 and retouched towards 1887

128 *Paysage aux Arbres*, 1884–5. In this black-lead drawing Seurat adopts a selective, analytical, discriminatory approach which is quite different from the earlier landscape-drawings, where continuity of tone is the essential. The trees to the right in the background of the *Grande Jatte* are seen here as nature first suggested them

any count that Seurat began 'the *picture*' at the same time as he began the sketches: except, that is, in so far as he regarded both the sixty-two sketches and the final picture as a single coherent enterprise. He was fortunate in that whereas Pissarro, for one, had to waste much of his time in scurrying round Paris in search of buyers who, as often as not, failed even to turn up for their appointments, Seurat could turbine away with the assurance that his income, though small, was secure. But the episode of the *Grande Jatte* is, none the less, even more remarkable, as a *tour de force* of concentration and high intent, than the episode of *Une Baignade, Asnières*.

129 *Arbres sur les Berges de la Seine*, 1884–5. A Conté crayon drawing in which
Seurat combines the analytical approach of *Ill. 128* with the closely argued tonal
procedures of earlier drawings. The trees stand in for human beings and the
Grande Jatte is already foreshadowed

130 *Nourrice Debout, un Enfant dans les Bras, c.* 1882. An early instance of Seurat's preoccupation with the nurse-and-child relationship: the nurse's apron and the child's dress become a single white form against which the nurse herself is outlined

CHAPTER FOUR

The Pan-Athenaic Frieze Brought Up to Date

As the *Grande Jatte* has been in the Chicago Art Institute since 1926, and is never likely to leave the building again, most enthusiasts can know it only at second or third hand. This is the more unfortunate in that reproduction cannot counterfeit the particular impact of the huge canvas. Nor can even those privileged to examine it *sur place* be sure that they have quite seized Seurat's intention, since the colour relations have undoubtedly deteriorated since the picture was painted. (As to the nature and extent of these changes, and the possibility of setting them partly to rights by varnishing, opinion was sharply divided, a year or two ago, and it was decided to take no action.)

When the *Grande Jatte* was first shown, in May 1886, it was regarded as a divisionist manifesto and Fénéon, for one, took it as a pretext for the elucidation of the new technique. But when seen in the 1960s it strikes the observer as decidedly incomplete in its adherence to divisionism. Later and smaller pictures make the case more clearly and cogently: what we see in the *Grande Jatte* is a further instance of multiple techniques, with divisionist passages alternating with passages of pure Impressionist brushwork. Nor does the picture now have the enhanced luminosity which was one of Seurat's objectives. As against this, however, the other qualities of the *Grande Jatte* are now more conspicuous than ever; of all the great poems-in-paint with which the French nineteenth century has dowered us it is one of the most arresting and the most mysterious.

Its immediate subject is clear enough. This is how Fénéon defined it: 'It is four o'clock on Sunday afternoon in the dog-days. On the river the swift barks dart to and fro. On the island itself, a Sunday population has come together at random, and from a delight in the fresh air, among the trees. Seurat has treated his forty or so figures in summary and hieratic style, setting them up frontally or with their backs to us or in profile, seated at right-angles, stretched out horizontally, or bolt upright: like a Puvis de Chavannes gone modern.'

All this is true, but it does not go far towards defining the fascination of the picture. Above all, Fénéon does not touch on the question which, in the 1960s, is perhaps most interesting of all: is the *Grande Jatte* primarily a work of direct social observation, or is it a late and marvellous instance of a kind of picture, the *poésie*, which was exemplified for Seurat in his formative days by such works in the Louvre as the Giorgione *Concert Champêtre* and the *Allegory* of Lorenzo Costa (*Ill. 149*)? Is it, that is to say, a realistic portrait of a transitional society? Or is it a product of the poetic imagination, and one whose meaning still eludes us?

131 *La Grande Jatte*, 1884–5. Of this uninhabited but relatively large-scale (25 by 32 inches) sketch, Roger-Marx wrote in 1884: 'Here is an art that is candid and sincere, and one that reveals a deep inner conviction not to be found, unhappily, among some of those who have taken to Impressionism'

132 Preliminary drawing for *La Grande Jatte*, 1884–5. Seurat sets, again on a substantial scale (15 by 23 inches), the stage which he will later populate: only the dog, as yet, has run ahead, and into just the place he will occupy in the finished picture

Both Seurat's choice of subject, and his method of work, are helpful in this context. For the *Grande Jatte* he returned to the scene of the *Baignade*: that long, thin, severed tongue of land in the middle of the Seine between Neuilly and Asnières. Once again the between-world fascinates him: the region that is neither town nor country. The subject combined two elements which were, in sociological terms, on the point of explosion: the industrial suburb and the industrial Sunday. It was conquerable country, in more senses than one: there were new places where pictures could hang (the mural in the town hall at Courbevoie was a commission that at least one of Seurat's friends put in for in 1884) and there were new social alignments to be studied, and new deformations of the social instinct to be set down as a warning, perhaps, to future generations. Unlike most painters, Seurat was a natural bookworm and there is every likelihood that he read those novels of the 1880s in which

133 *Un Dimanche d'été à l'Ile de la Grande Jatte*: painted between March 1884 and March 1885, taken up again in October 1885, completed in the spring of 1886, and put on show on 15th May 1886

Zola and J. K. Huysmans did pioneer work in charting the life of places comparable to Asnières and Courbevoie.

There is no doubt that he spent a great deal of time *sur le motif* on the island itself; and later, when he was dead and famous, his friends remembered all manner of picturesque details—how he had been too preoccupied even to greet them as they passed, how he had asked them to cut the grass at the water's edge when it grew too long, and how he had lunched off a bar of chocolate when summer was drawing in and he needed to finish his notes from nature.

In the main, these first-hand notes relate to nature: not to human beings. Seurat's tendency (exemplified above all in the uninhabited landscape in the John Hay Whitney collection, *Ill. 131*) was to give the Ile de la Grande Jatte its Monday face; later, when getting on to the big picture, he would people the island as he pleased. This means that at no point do we see the island as it really was at four o'clock on a Sunday afternoon in high summer; for as his first biographer, Gustave Coquiot, says: 'Seurat was too sedate to like the Grande Jatte as it really was on a Sunday. His famous picture is very well composed, but it shows a Grande Jatte that has gone prim and level-headed and lost its appetites.' For the island at this time was both a genuine working-class background and a place to which fashionables and persons of consequence liked to come on the sly. For Seurat's fastidious purposes much of the tumult, rowdiness, disorder, bawdry and violent physical exertion had first to be drawn off from the scene. (Coquiot complained that Seurat presented 'a Sacred Wood with neither nymphs nor Priapus'.) But this did not mean either a descent into gentility or a flight from the modern world: on the contrary, Seurat contrived to make a picture which is unmistakably of the 1880s and yet valid, as a portrait of society, for all time.

The more we look at this painting, the more evident are its departures from the naturalistic ideal. It employs, for instance, multiple perspective. If we were to examine it from the point of view of unified Renaissance perspective, with the painter's stool squarely before the centre of the canvas and a foot or two in front of it, it would follow that the two people in the foreground on the right would be very tall indeed; the people on the left would be

134 *La Nounou*, 1884–5. In this Conté crayon drawing the nurse's back and shoulders carry over the form (see *Ill. 34*) of one of Seurat's haystacks

dwarfs, save for the reclining pipe-smoker. The whole of this foreground zone is, in fact, seen from a point on the extreme right of the canvas; when we emerge into the sunlight, in the middleground, this is no longer the case. On the Seine, the wind is blowing from two quarters at once: from the right, in the case of the left-hand steamer and sailboat, and from the left, in the case of those farther to the right. Certain of the forms correspond not so much to 'common sense' as to recurrent preoccupations of the artist. That the old woman with her back to us in the left-hand middleground is, in effect, a haystack with a hat on it (*Ill. 134*), I have already pointed out; but just above and to the left of her that same form, the flattened cone, reappears in the mound on which the fisherman is sitting.

135 *Paysage et Personnages*, 1884–5. Before he needed to monumentalize the whole conception of the *Grande Jatte* Seurat was able, as here, to complete oil-sketches in which he reverted to the searching, flickering, criss-crossed brush-strokes of earlier days

136 *Promeneuse*, *c*. 1882. Conté crayon drawing

The portable stove (extreme right) has a monumental quality which cannot be accidental. Never a great physiognomist (or rather: too busy with an emblematic conception of bearing and dress to bother with the particularities of human feature), Seurat has not characterized the majority of his figures; but the pipe-smoker (left foreground) is painted with a realism not paralleled anywhere else in the painting.

Seurat did not care to be pressed for literary or symbolic elucidations of the *Grande Jatte*, claiming rather that he had just taken the

137 *Promeneuse au Réverbère*, *c*. 1882. Conté crayon drawing

138 *Femmes au Bord de l'Eau, c.* 1885–6. Dorra and Rewald suggest that although the subject-matter of this little oil-panel is very closely related to that of the *Grande Jatte*, its pointillist execution would indicate that it is an independent work, and it may have been

executed later than the big picture. But it may also be that Seurat wished to experiment with the effect in this particular context of a technique closer to pure divisionism than any he had employed hitherto

139–42 Four examples of Seurat's treatment of the single figure in his Conté crayon drawings: 139 (*left*) *Le Nœud Noir*, c. 1882; 140 (*right*) *Femme Debout, la Tête Nue*, c. 1882

subject that was nearest to hand. ('If I'd wanted to', he said, 'I could just as well have painted the struggle between the Horatii and Curiatii.') But so much of modern life was deliberately brought into the picture that we cannot regard it quite in this light. It seems very probable that he drew upon fashion-plates of the time for certain costumes. (Mr Benedict Nicolson has pointed to the striking similarity between the elegant couple in the foreground to the right of the *Grande Jatte* and the figures which stand for the latest high fashion in Walter Crane's *A Fantasy of Fashion, 1837–1887*.) No less evident, to my eye, is the reference to the cartoons of Léonce Petit in *Le Journal Amusant*: it cannot be an accident that not long previously Petit had published *Plaisirs du dimanche: la promenade sur le Cours*, a cartoon of which the lower half has elements repeated almost identically in the *Grande Jatte*. Striking, too, are the parallels be-

141 (left) *Artiste*, c. 1882; 142 (right) *Nourrice*, c. 1882

tween the *Grande Jatte* and more than one passage in the *avant-garde* literature of the 1880s. Seurat was not in any sense an illustrative artist: but he had met Mallarmé in 1884, and it seems improbable that there was no interaction between the two at the time when Seurat was completing the *Grande Jatte* and Mallarmé was producing, in 1884, *Prose pour des Esseintes* and, in June–July 1885, *Le Nénuphar Blanc*. In both of Mallarmé's pieces island imagery predominates; and *Le Nénuphar Blanc*, with its rowing trip on the Seine, and its boat stranded on a marshy island, '*cette obstacle de verdure en pointe sur le courant*', could relate partly to gossip among Seurat's friends about the enormous picture in progress.

Fénéon's pioneer article on the *Grande Jatte* stressed above all the novelty and significance of its use of colour. But today, when the resources of colour have been pushed a great deal further, what

155

143 *Groupes de Personnages*, 1884–5. An early sketch for the *Grande Jatte*, in which Seurat has not yet adopted the plunging viewpoint of the final picture and has allowed the foliage a degree of more prominence and variety which he later retracted

impresses us is, rather, Seurat's determination to compose in terms of perfect spatial harmony, and his belief that harmony could be achieved consciously. It may be meaningful, in this context, that Seurat hung the huge canvas on his studio-wall, working at it from a pair of steps. As Wittkower once said: 'A wall [at the time of the Renaissance] is seen as a unit which contains certain harmonic potentialities. The lowest sub-units into which the whole unit can be broken up are the consonant intervals of the musical scale, the cosmic validity of which was not doubted.'

The *Grande Jatte* is one of those great pictures in which every generation finds the meaning best suited to it. In its beginnings, Verhaeren regarded it as '*un essai décisif dans la recherche de la plus vraie lumière*': others harked back to Egypt, or Assyria, or Benozzo Gozzoli, or harked across to Kate Greenaway, in their attempts to bring the canvas somehow within the frontiers of the familiar: and

Seurat himself thought rather of the Pan-Athenaic procession on the Parthenon—as much, one may think, for its abundance of human types as for its frieze-like disposition. To Roger Fry, in 1926, it represented 'a world from which life and movement are banished and all is fixed for ever in the rigid frame of its geometry'. For Robert Rey, in 1931, it impressed by its nearness to that novelty of a later day, the slow-motion film. Meyer Schapiro in 1935 was the first to glimpse the profundity of Seurat's social insights: 'Never through calculation and geometrical designing alone,' he wrote, 'could Seurat arrive at a painting with the qualities, *even the formal qualities*' [my italics] 'of the *Grande Jatte*.' In 1949 E. M. Forster put the subject at the level it deserves when he wrote that 'Art . . . is the one orderly product which our muddling race has produced. It is the cry of a thousand sentinels, the echo from a thousand labyrinths; it is the

144 *Figures Assises*, 1884–5. Here again, a great deal needed to be done on the tree that stands just right of centre, and the boy in the foreground has strayed in from *Une Baignade, Asnières*. But as Professor Rewald points out, this is a sketch in which the chosen section of the site and the position of the sun are those Seurat used in the final picture

145 *La Jeune Fille dans l'Atelier, c.* 1887

lighthouse which cannot be hidden: *c'est le meilleur témoignage que nous puissions donner de notre dignité.* "Antigone" for "Antigone's" sake, "Macbeth" for "Macbeth's", "La Grande Jatte" for "La Grande Jatte's".' To Meyer Schapiro, again, what was most striking in 1958 was 'the range of qualities and content within the same work: from the articulated and formed to its ground in the relatively homogeneous dots; an austere construction, yet so much of nature and human life; the cool observer, occupied with his abstruse problems of art, and the common world of the crowds and amusements of Paris; the exact mind, fanatic about its methods and theories, and the poetic visionary, absorbed in contemplating the mysterious light and shadow of a transfigured domain . . .' H. W.

146 *La Pêcheuse à la Ligne*, 1884–5. One of the most elegant of the preparatory drawings for the *Grande Jatte*

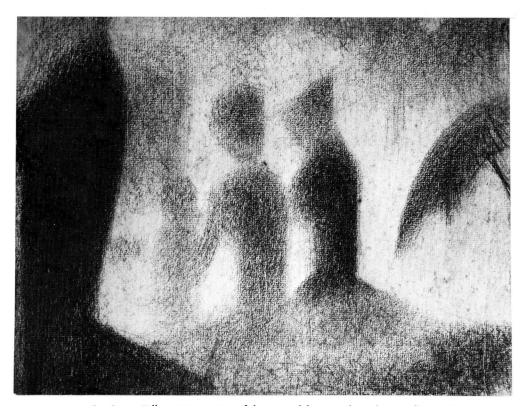

147 *Les Jeunes Filles*, 1884–5. One of the most delicate and tenebrous of Seurat's drawings for the seated girls in the *Grande Jatte*, and for the umbrellas which figure in it

Janson added the significance of the monkey, in medieval times, as a symbol of profligacy. Today we mark out the compositional axes, wrangle from time to time about the sociological implications, and dig ever deeper into the source-material which arose transmogrified at Seurat's bidding. But to me the picture remains the latest and the last of the *poesie* with which, after Giorgione's example, painters have endowed us. In Seurat's almost musical devotion to the exact interval, the key-structure of light and colour which will suit his purpose; in the introduction (in a pose adapted from an antique bronze) of the strolling trumpeter by the water's edge; in the rapt, still, unconversational portrait of a world in which 'life itself is conceived as a sort of listening', and in the way in which we are reminded of how, to quote Pater, 'from music, the school of Gior-

148 *Sept Singes*, 1884–5. One of four sheets of drawings of monkeys which have survived. Seurat would not seem to have found in nature the exquisite emblematic form which he adopted, in the finished painting, for the monkey's tail

149 The Louvre's *Allegory*, 62 by 76 inches, by Lorenzo Costa

gione passes often to the play which is like music; to those masques
in which men avowedly do but play at real life, like children
"dressing up", disguised in the strange old Italian dresses, parti-
coloured or fantastic with embroidery and furs, of which the master
was so curious a designer . . .' —in all this, surely, there is a case
for seeing the *Grande Jatte* as the heir to one of the great poetic
traditions of European painting. Strike out 'Italian' from Pater's
evocation, and it could have been written with Seurat in mind.

This interpretation seems to me the more plausible in that Seurat
must often have seen, during his visits to the Louvre, a painting
which has curious affinities with *La Grande Jatte*. This is the *Allegory*,
as it is now called (*Ill. 149*), by Lorenzo Costa (1460–1535). In Seurat's

150 (*right*) *Couple se Promenant*, 1884–5. In the final painting the shadows cast (not
always quite logically) by the trees are a good deal less emphatic than in this oil-sketch

151 *Esquisse d'Ensemble*, 1884–5. Whereas for *Une Baignade, Asnières* no penultimate draft exists, for the *Grande Jatte* Seurat made this ensemble sketch at roughly one-third the size of the final version. In colour it goes a good deal further than that final version. Seurat seems,

however, to have decided that this was the maximum size at which strict divisionist principles could be followed; and for the painterly eloquence of this *esquisse d'ensemble* he later
substituted majestic organizational power and a wealth of closely observed social detail

152 *Fillette au Chapeau Niniche*, c. 1883. A classic instance of how Seurat could minimize all physical references in the interests of an ideal purity in the contrast of black with white and light with dark

day it was known as *The Court of Isabella d'Este, Duchess of Mantua*, and Frédéric Villot's catalogue-entry includes an elaborate key to the action: in a riverside garden Isabella d'Este is being crowned by Love, personified by a small boy who stands upright on the knees of a white-robed woman seated on the stump of a tree. Musicians play, meanwhile, and poets write verses in her honour. In the foreground two women crown a bull and a lamb with flowers, and near by is a bare-breasted nymph with bow and arrows. In the foreground on the left a warrior (identified by some critics with Balthazar Castiglione) leans on the halberd with which he has just cut off the head of a hydra. In the distance is a combat of cavaliers and a galleon at anchor.

153 *L'Enfant Blanc*, 1884–5. Many years before Malevich thought of painting 'white on white', Seurat achieved in this domain a ghostly intensity. In this drawing for the little girl in the *Grande Jatte* he did not adumbrate the face, as he does in the painting, but the fragility of the arms, and of the body beneath the dress, comes through very strongly

Villot's interpretation has since been contested, and Edgar Wind, for one, has seen the painting rather as a 'Jardin d'Harmonie'. There is no reason to suppose that Seurat bothered himself with the 'meaning' of the picture, but there are a number of striking similarities between the two works. There is, to begin with, a kindred unreality about the two painters' use of perspective: Costa's figures weave in and out of strict perspective in obedience to the poetic impulse behind them, and so do Seurat's. Seurat's solitary trumpeter corresponds to Costa's string-players, his tug-boat to Costa's galleon, and the strenuous activity of his four oarsmen to Costa's emblematic battle. The slender walking-stick so fastidiously held by the top-hatted man on the grass answers to the warrior's halberd, even,

154 *Petite Esquisse pour 'La Grande Jatte'* 1884–5. An oil-sketch midway, one may think, between the natural disorder of the scene itself and the thought-out and constructed dignity of the final painting

and the element of fancy-dress in Costa has its counterpart in Seurat's meaningful fashion-notes. It may not be by accident that Seurat, like Costa, closes the upper left-hand side of his composition with an upward thrust of foliage, or that the light on the embankment on the far side of the Seine forms a horizontal streak of pallor comparable to that on the far side of Costa's inlet. Janson's theory about Seurat's monkey would bring it into line with the bull and the lamb in Costa. Even the reeds at the water's edge, in both canvases, could be said to have affinities. So could the row of tree-trunks which, in Costa as in Seurat, serve to mark out the space to right of centre. Altogether there is evidence enough to suggest that Seurat may have had Costa present in his mind, as a poetic idea, along with all the other people and things which went to the making of one of the greatest of all French paintings.

155 *Arbre et Homme*, 1884–5. The man on the bank plays only a tiny part in the final painting, and his presence there has none of the brooding, almost menacing, quality which distinguishes it here. But the drawing of the tree is one of the finest instances of Seurat's ability to refine and simplify the forms with which nature presented him

156 *Petite Esquisse*, 1884–5. Seurat here cuts off that vital section at the extreme right of the final painting in which the tall standing human figures and the undecorated tree-trunks raise and lighten what could be called the ceiling of the picture; but for painterly quality this is one of the most delicious of the sketches

The Société des Artistes Indépendants was an artists' collective, with annual dues, a triennial share-out, and an ideally democratic constitution. Its basic idea was to break the power of the State, on the one hand, and of the dealers on the other, and to give the artist more of a say in his own destiny. Dear as all this was to the founders, it was no guarantee of practical success: the second show, in December 1884, was miserably attended and the third, scheduled for March 1885, did not take place at all. Seurat, punctual as a Swiss express, had his big picture ready in time; and when the show fell through he decided to take some time off, after his ten months' continuous exertion, and went to stay by the sea, at Grandcamp, on the Normandy coast. From this visit dates the beginning of his marine activities.

157 *Couple se Promenant*, 1884–5. A Conté crayon drawing which, if taken together with *Ill. 156*, would furnish almost all the compositional material from
which the final painting was built up

158 *Deux Voiliers à Grandcamp*, oil on canvas, 1885

The little panels that survive (most of them six inches by ten) are mostly painted on a plain ground with horizontal dabs of pure colour that derive more from late Impressionism than from divisionist practice. In one of them a rearing form (*Ill. 158*) forecasts the motif of *Le Bec du Hoc à Grandcamp* (*Ill. 159*), but in general they are tentative, carefully zoned colour-notes in which hull and sail and steep-roofed hut serve to mark out space and create spatial tension, much as houses and haystacks had done in Seurat's earlier panels. But when he came to work up his ideas on canvas he proceeded quite differently. In *Le Bec du Hoc* (*Ill. 159*), for instance, he tapered the paint-area very slightly, towards the top; he included, above the central motif, an emblematic group of sea-birds; and, as in *Marée Basse à Grandcamp* (ChH 155), he painted the edges of the canvas with specklings that complemented the scene within. In the Whitney *Grandcamp, Un Soir* (*Ill. 160*) (a painting omitted by de Hauke) he took

172

the descending line, from left to right, that first appeared in the *Baignade* and varied it not with a group of figures but with an attention, at first sight quite undeserved, to the verticals, the horizontals, and the white-squared diagonal of the wall and staircase in the left foreground. In the *Fort-Samson à Grandcamp* (*Ill. 161*), there appears above the rug-like dunes the mysterious, equivocal cone-shape that he had used in his earlier panels; and in another large experimental canvas, the *Rade de Grandcamp* (*Ill. 163*) Seurat again combined motifs from the pre-*Baignade* era with a new freedom and independence of convention. These are divisionist pictures, in a sense, but they do not give the vivid, saturated, never-contaminated radiance for which the

159 *Le Bec du Hoc à Grandcamp*, oil on canvas, 1885

160 *Grandcamp, Un Soir*, oil on canvas, 1885

pioneers were striving. On the contrary, the general effect is subdued
and dim: appropriate enough, perhaps, to the muffled *temps couvert*
of the Normandy coast.

   On his return to Paris, Seurat seems to have reworked the *Grande
Jatte* in a divisionist direction (*Ill. 164*). (The large uninhabited
island-scape, *Ill. 131*, was also reworked.) He may have been led
to penetrate further into this specific problem by the enthusiasm of
certain new-found admirers, senior among whom was Camille
Pissarro, then aged fifty-five. Pissarro was at a point of crisis in
his own career which made him particularly responsive to new ideas,

and from his letters to his son Lucien we have the vividest impression of what it was like to come under Seurat's spell. It was thanks to Pissarro's lobbying, above all, that Seurat and Signac were able to contribute to the eighth and last Impressionist exhibition, the first since 1862, which was held in May–June 1886. And with the appearance in that show of the *Grande Jatte*, the *Bec du Hoc*, and four other paintings, Seurat became one of the most talked-of painters of the day.

'Talked-of' but not always admired: Seurat had to face not only public ridicule but the envy and hatred which are never far beneath the surface of the inner art-world. His admission had caused trouble from the first: as Pissarro said, 'the old, romantic Impressionists have every interest in fighting the new tendencies. I accept the fact that it has to come to a fight. But they are trying to ruin the exhibition

161 *Le Fort Samson à Grandcamp*, oil on panel, 1885

before it's even on the wall.' These disagreements were plain enough at the Impressionists' dinner in March 1886, where Pissarro defended Seurat before Huysmans, Monet, Mallarmé, George Moore and others; and when the show was on, Seurat was drawn into discourtesies which he regretted (the boycotting, for instance, of Degas' visit) and quarrels from which he withdrew himself as best he could. (When Guillaumin claimed that seniority should have entitled him to a place at the head of the new movement, Seurat 'just shut his mouth and ducked behind a newspaper'.) There was also a brush with Gauguin: Seurat, thinking to defend Signac's interests, had forbidden Gauguin to use Signac's studio. The episode, trifling in itself, is significant for the terms of Gauguin's retort: 'I may be a hesitant and unlearned artist, but as a man of the world I allow no one to mess me about.' 'Hesitant and unlearned' was doubtless meant to contrast with the already famous assurance, and the profound historical sense, which underlay Seurat's activity.

That activity was received by the press with almost uniform derision. But one article marked, on the contrary, the beginnings of an authoritative understanding of Seurat and his friends. This was contributed to *La Vogue* by Félix Fénéon, and although it appeared just at the moment when the exhibition in the rue Laffitte was closing it remained for many years, and in fact is still today, the classic presentation of Seurat's ideas.

Fénéon was one of the most remarkable figures of his day. Not quite twenty-five at the time his article appeared, he had been an enthusiast for Seurat ever since he had seen the *Baignade* in 1884. During office hours he was a model employee, as it seemed, of the War Ministry: General Boulanger himself had minuted his dossier with the words 'Fénéon can be counted upon'. But the people who could really count on Fénéon, over the next forty or fifty years, were the new talents of the day. Jean Paulhan put the case for Fénéon when he wrote: 'We have had, perhaps, only one critic in the last hundred years: Félix Fénéon. He it was who in 1883 preferred Rimbaud to all the other poets of the day; who from 1884 onwards stood up for Verlaine and Huysmans, Charles Cros and Moréas, Marcel Schwob and Alfred Jarry; who then discovered Seurat,

Gauguin, Cézanne and Van Gogh. As editor of the *Revue Blanche* from 1895 to 1903—yes, from 1895 to 1903!—he published Gide and Proust, Apollinaire and Claudel, Renard and Péguy, Bonnard, Vuillard, Debussy, Roussel, Matisse . . .'

Even if it is too much to say that in any but a private sense Fénéon 'discovered' Cézanne, Gauguin and Van Gogh he did undoubtedly discover Seurat, as far as the intelligent public was concerned. As a very old man he wrote to John Rewald that he had been aware, from the start, of the importance of the *Baignade*: 'the masterpieces which were its logical consequence followed one after the other; but, much as I delighted in them, the initial spice of surprise was never repeated.'

162 *Couché sous un Pont,* Conté crayon, *c.* 1885

163 *La Rade de Grand-camp*, 1885. Sails here play the part which, in landscape done at Le Raincy and elsewhere, was assigned to the angles of roofs and corner-turrets and garden-walls. For the sea, as against the grass and the leafage in the foreground, Seurat still kept to a late-Impressionist handling

178

There must, even so, have been spice of another sort about the first meetings between Seurat and Fénéon. Tradition has it that these took place in front of the *Grande Jatte* in the rue Laffitte and that Fénéon's article was a faithful account of what Seurat had told him. Authoritative it certainly was: but a glance at the rest of the article, or at any other of Fénéon's writings, will show that he was quite capable of making up his mind for himself and of getting his facts right. His few lines on Berthe Morisot are the joy and despair of all others who attempt to write about her. By the time, in short, that we get to the 'innovators', Fénéon has established himself among the rare great writers on art.

The passage is worth quoting in full:

'From the beginning, the Impressionist painters were impelled by their regard for truth to limit themselves to the interpretation of modern life directly observed and landscape directly painted. They saw objects as interdependent, each participating, where light was concerned, in the practices of their neighbours, where traditional painting had considered them each on its own and had lit them with a light that was meagre and artificial.

'This interaction of colour, these sudden perceptions of complementaries, this Japanese vision could not be expressed by means of dark sauces worked up on the palette: these artists made, therefore, distinct and isolated colour-notations, allowing their colours to vibrate with emotion at their brusque contacts with one another. When seen from a distance, those same colours would harmonize, envelop the subject of the painting in light and air, modelling the forms in light and going so far sometimes as to forgo modelling altogether: sunshine itself was caught on the canvas.

'The Impressionists practised, that is to say, the decomposition of colour; but they practised it in an arbitrary fashion: sometimes the full brush would move across the canvas and leave behind it the sensation of red; sometimes a glowing passage was cross-hatched with green. MM. Georges Seurat, Camille and Lucien Pissarro, Dubois-Pillet and Signac are painters who, on the contrary, practise divisionism consciously and scientifically. This procedure they developed in 1884, 1885 and 1886.

'If, in M. Seurat's *Grande Jatte*, you take a small patch of uniform tone, you will find that it is made up of a whirling host of tiny dots, and that those dots spell out the constituent elements of the tone. Take the shaded grass: most of the brush-strokes give the local value of the grass; others, orange in tone, are scattered here and there to stand for the almost imperceptible action of the sun; other dots, purple in colour, introduce the complementary of green; where a patch of grass lies nearer to the sunshine, a cyanine blue comes into action, grows thicker and thicker as we approach the line of demarcation, and dies away on the far side of it. When we come to the grass that is actually in the sun, two elements only are concerned: green, and the sunbeam's orange. The light, here, is too violent for any interaction to be possible. Black being a non-light, the black dog takes on the colours thrown up from the grass: predominant among these is, therefore, a dark purple; but the dog is also attacked by a dark blue, the product of near-by areas of light. The monkey on a lead is spotted with yellow, which is its own personal colour, and speckled also with purple and ultramarine. All this is a matter, as will be all too clear, of clumsy indications, when one tries to put it into words; but when you see it on the canvas the delicacy and complexity of the gauging involved are immediately clear.

'Isolated on the canvas, these colours re-compose on the retina: what we have is not, therefore, a mingling of colours conceived in terms of pigment. It is a mingling of colours conceived in terms of light. I need hardly say that, where the same colours are involved, a mingling of pigments does not necessarily give the same results as a mingling of light-rays. We also know that the luminosity of an optical mingling is always very much greater than the luminosity of a material mingling of pigments. The many equations of luminosity established by M. Rood prove this decisively. For carmine violet and Prussian blue, from which a grey-blue emerges:

$$\frac{50 \text{ carmine} + 50 \text{ blue}}{\text{mingling of pigments}} = \frac{47 \text{ carmine} + 49 \text{ blue} + 4 \text{ black}}{\text{mingling of light-rays}}$$

for carmine and green:

$$50 \text{ carmine} + 50 \text{ green} = 50 \text{ carmine} + 24 \text{ green} + 26 \text{ black}$$

'It will now be easy to see why, in their struggle to express a maximum of luminosity, the Impressionists (like Delacroix before them) wanted to substitute an optical mingling for a mingling of pigments on the palette.

'Georges Seurat is the first man to present a complete and systematic paradigm of this new way of painting. Wherever you choose to examine it, his enormous painting, the *Grande Jatte*, will unroll before you like some patient, monotonous, myriad-speckled tapestry. This is a kind of painting in which cheating is impossible and "stylish handling" quite pointless. There is no room in it for the bravura piece. The hand may go numb, but the eye must remain agile, learned and perspicacious. Whether the subject is an ostrich, a bundle of straw, a wave or a rock, the movement of the brush remains the same. One could argue that when it comes to rendering coarse grasses, or branches astir in the wind, or the heavy coat of an animal, there are advantages in the contrasting sabre-cuts and suavities of traditional "fine painting": but the pointillist technique is clearly superior for the rendering of smooth surfaces and, in particular, for the nude, a subject to which it has not yet been applied.'

After describing the subject of the picture in terms which I have already quoted, Fénéon went on to say: 'The atmosphere is transparent and has a peculiar vibration: the surface of the picture seems to move to and fro before our eyes. This sensation may be explicable according to the theory of Dove: once warned that whole clusters of points of light, each distinct from the other, are in operation against it, the retina takes cognizance, in the rapidest possible alternation, both of the individual colour-elements, in isolation, and of the combinations which result when they re-assemble.'

The point of this article is that it is an immensely intelligent presentation of views which Fénéon learnt from, or at any rate checked with, Seurat himself. These are, therefore, the terms in which Seurat wanted to have the picture discussed. The important thing was to establish divisionism as a serious activity—and an activity which arose logically from the position into which painting had got itself. That this was so soon taken for granted by the people who really

(*right*) A detail from the *Grande Jatte*. Seurat had re-worked it, in certain respects, on his return from Grandcamp

165 *Bout de la Jetée à Honfleur*, 1886. Seurat remarked in a letter to Signac on the dull, hooded weather in which he worked on this picture

counted in Paris was the achievement of Fénéon almost as much as of Seurat. By the time, in any case, that Seurat left for Honfleur in the second half of June 1886 he had affected in one way or another a whole Pléiade of painters: Camille Pissarro and his son Lucien, Signac, Van Gogh, Angrand, H. E. Cross, Anquetin, Emile Bernard, Emile Schuffenecker, and Theo van Rysselberghe. Fénéon, Verhaeren and Gustave Kahn were the more prominent among his writer-friends. He had 'pierced', as the French say, on every front; but more eloquent than any written tribute is the sheer borrowed stringency of a painting like Signac's *The Seine at Les Andelys*

184

(1886) and the delicate organization of Pissarro's *Early Morning, Rouen* (1888), where the play of verticals and horizontals and right angles and the wraith-like quality of the dotted forms derive directly from Seurat. No less touching, in this context, is Van Gogh's persistence in seeking out subjects similar to those that Seurat had treated.

These allegiances brought mixed comfort, however, to Seurat himself. In one sense, he invited them by stressing the methodical, Cartesian element in his activity. In another, he very much disliked

166 *Entrée du Port à Honfleur*, 1866. One of the grandest and most cogent of all Seurat's *marines*, carried out throughout on pure divisionist principles and making use of harbour-architecture in a way not to be paralleled until Seurat's sojourn at Gravelines in 1890

167 *La 'Maria' à Honfleur*, 1886. The play of verticals in this painting is as subtle as anything in Seurat, as is also the constantly varying intensity with which he registers the furniture of the quayside

the idea that others might ride to success on his back and he felt, quite rightly, that the dot, on which everyone seized, was only one of the elements of his success. It was soon to be proved, positively by himself, negatively by others, that the dot could only be used in memorable style by an artist with quite exceptional powers of organization and the painter's equivalent of 'perfect pitch'.

These qualities came out strongly in the work done by Seurat at Honfleur in 1886. These are the first paintings in which Seurat used the dot throughout as the main instrument of expression: and, in addition, they display that quality of the non-accidental which had

168 *Coin d'un Bassin, Honfleur*, 1886. Seurat only worked for eight days on this painting, and he considered it rather as a big sketch than as a finished painting. Although he signed it and sent it to the Indépendants in 1886 it is probable that, given time and the opportunity, he would have re-worked it in the discriminating idiom of *Ill. 167*

169 *Le Peintre au Travail, c.* 1884. There is no warrant for calling this a self-portrait, but the formal dress, the measured elegance of the stance, and the equally measured concentration on a huge canvas—all accord with our knowledge of Seurat.

hitherto been obscured by the oddity of his subject-matter and the intrusive curiosity of the dot. In the Kröller-Müller *Bout de La Jetée, Honfleur (Ill. 165)*, the strongest single accent is that of the bollard to the extreme right of the picture. In the Barnes *Entrée du Port (Ill. 166)* the capstan in the immediate foreground is so placed that not merely a length of cable but Seurat's whole composition can be controlled by it; and in the Prague *Maria, Honfleur (Ill. 167)* and the Kröller-Müller *Coin d'un Bassin (Ill. 168)* Seurat put the new knowledge of ships and their equipment which he had learnt from Signac to purposes which, once again, are not those of 'realism'.

170 *Écluse dans Paris, c.* 1884. Like many of Seurat's drawings, this reminds us of how much he admired Whistler as a man who knew how to use the night as material for his art

171 *L'Embouchure de la Seine, Un Soir, Honfleur*. One of the most melancholic of all Seurat's *marines*, with the cluster of verticals on the left to offset the picture's one romantic outline (that of the rock on the right)

Seurat was starting, in short, to bring to the delineation of a given scene the apparatus of certainty which had gone out of European painting with the death of Poussin; and one cannot better, in this context, the list of Poussin's devices which Sir Kenneth Clark once drew up: 'The measured interplay of horizontals and verticals, the use of a house, a window, or a block of masonry as a modulus of proportion, the diagonal which turns back on itself after two-thirds of its journey, the arc whose ideated centre is a nodal point in the comparison . . .'

It was not merely to the history of art that Seurat related these preoccupations. He and his friends really believed that a new era in human consciousness was at hand. They lived, after all, at a time when power, in one new form or another, was coming ever more under human control; when knowledge seemed to lead uninterruptedly to wisdom; and when our conscious command of existence was changing more, and more rapidly, than at any time in history. The classic text, in this connection, is a sentence which occurred in an article by Charles Henry in the *Revue Philosophique*. Henry's is now a forgotten name, but at one time, and to people as various as Signac and Paul Valéry, Seurat and Jules Laforgue, he seemed one of the cleverest men alive. His investigations extended into a great many departments of life, and one principle he deduced from them was this: that 'certain phenomena which, for ourselves, are the affair of

172 *La Grève du Bas Butin à Honfleur*, 1886. As in *Ill. 171*, Seurat here composes his picture in terms of a lapsed diagonal, with the vegetation, in this case, thrown like a rug across the irregular contour of the cliff and the breakwater-posts once again vital to the design

consciousness were unconscious at an epoch as near to our own as the Greco-Roman. Human beings are, therefore, incontestably progressing towards a state of ever-greater life-enhancement.'

In Henry's view, and in Seurat's, the elements of that enhancement could be defined where painting was concerned. (But this is not to say that Henry, any more than Seurat, was the captive of his theories. In this context an entry in Signac's diary for December 1894 is relevant: 'Charles Henry came to see me. He is getting to be more and more poetical. He will start from an exact and scientific premise, and from it he will draw the most delightfully whimsical conclusions. Then he tries to find mathematical proofs for them . . .'). Already in 1884 Henry had lectured at the Sorbonne on the emotional signifi-cance of colour and line. Certain colours, certain mathematical pro-portions, certain arrangements of line, were more enhancing than others: or, to preserve Henry's language exactly, some were *dynamo-gènes*, others *inhibitoires*. As to which was which, in what degree, science could tell exactly. For instance, upward movements and movements from left to right were dynamogenic; downward movements and movements from right to left were inhibitory. Red and yellow had a positive, green, violet and blue a relatively negative effect. With the help of a chromatic circle (a project with which Signac gave Henry much practical assistance) all ranks of society could learn to see correctly and well. And, more than this, a science of num-bers could be evolved: something which would combine the *arit-metica universalis* for which Paul Valéry later sought with the number-ratios implicit in Alberti and Palladio and the notion, widely current in the Paris of the 1880s, of a universally applicable grammar of sensory experience. For Henry was, in intention at least, a panto-math: ear and eye had yielded already, his friends thought, to his doctrines: palate and nose would follow suit, and eventually every department of modern life would be changed for the better.

Water would be turned into petrol, even; binoculars, made to Henry's specification, would automatically correct and suppress sensations inimical to his intents; archaeology, the objective sciences and the art of war would all feel his impact. And Henry pushed forward into speculations which, to some, now seem to foreshadow

173 *(right)* La Tour Eiffel, 1889. In painting the Eiffel Tower before it was even completed, Seurat struck a blow for modernity. The Tower in its first youth was covered with iridiscent enamel paint in several colours; and, as Meyer Schapiro once pointed out, it 'offers a formal resemblance to the art of Seurat'

Planck's quantum theory and the notion of cosmic radiation; his activities also included the discovery and editing of unpublished manuscripts of Stendhal and the compilation of a table of ratios for the habitual player of roulette.

Where painting was concerned, much of this merely confirmed what Seurat had decided upon both from his knowledge of earlier writers and from his own observations. The value of Henry's activity lay first in the climate of excitement and optimism which it produced and second in its assurance that advances in the conscious control of the material of art would be paralleled by advance in a great many other fields as well. 'Do you think', Seurat would ask Gustave Kahn, 'that there are correspondences between my innovations and those of Wagner?' And Charles Henry was able to reassure him that he was, in effect, the standard-bearer of a new and more rational form of beauty.

174 *Garçonnet Assis*, Conté crayon drawing, *c.* 1884

175 *La Poseuse, de Face*, 1887. A sketch for the central figure in *Les Poseuses*

CHAPTER FIVE

Master-Subjects In and Out of Doors

Seurat was not, of course, the only painter to seek, in the mid-1880s, a more systematic use of colour and line. (Gauguin, early in 1885, had been groping towards a physiology of aesthetics: in January 1885 he wrote to Pissarro from Copenhagen: 'Why is it that the willow whose branches incline downwards is called the weeper? Is it because there is something sad about a line that moves downwards?') But the uniqueness of Seurat's contribution lay in the fact that, having first learnt to construct his colour harmonies according to fixed laws of physics and optics, he went on to submit the other elements of the picture—design, structure, line, and the distribution of movement and force—to laws equally stringent. The great pictures of his last years—the *Poseuses* (1887), the *Parade* (1887–8), *Chahut* (1889–90), the unfinished *Cirque* (1891), and to a large degree the later landscapes as well—were all conceived and carried out in this way. He was still capable of undirected observations as brilliant and original as those manifested in his earlier drawings. But many of these (the elaborate groupings, for instance, of the drawing called *Condoléances* (*Ill. 177*) and the wonderfully sumptuous drawings of café-concerts (*Ill. 204*)) were never worked up as paintings; and where drawing-subjects did get carried over, as happened with certain studies of dancers, tumblers and barkers, there was usually a loss of particularity. When he chose to give a cut from urban life, Seurat could do it as decisively as Daumier: there are passages even in the *Grande Jatte* to prove this, and drawings as various as the two *Promenade* studies (*Ills. 136–7*), the *Lecture, 1883–4* (though this, *Ill. 58*, looks rather forward to Vuillard than back to Daumier), and the *Strapontin* (CdH 615). But this was not his aim at Grandcamp or at Honfleur: nor was it his aim in the *Poseuses*, which occupied him from the autumn of 1886 to the spring of 1888.

177 *Condoléances*, Conté crayon, *c.* 1886

This picture (*Ill. 187*) was painted in Seurat's studio on the fifth floor of 128b, Boulevard de Clichy. It raises, among many other problems, the question of Seurat's use of space and perspective. The scene is a corner of the studio. The wall to the left is covered almost entirely with as much of the *Grande Jatte* as could be got into the painter's field of vision. On the right-hand wall are four other, much smaller, pictures: not, probably, the specimens of Guys, Forain and Guillaumin which some of Seurat's friends remembered; nor, certainly, the poster by Chéret which marked one of his greatest enthusiasms: but most likely, white-framed *croquetons* of his own. In the lower left corner is the red divan, in the lower right corner the frugal stove, familiar from eye-witness accounts. The three *poseuses* are seen

176 (*left*) *Femme Assise sous les Arbres*, Conté crayon, *c.* 1882

178 *La Poseuse Debout*, 1887. A drawing in Conté crayon, perceptibly more explicit in its anatomical detail than any of the oil-paintings devoted to the subject

179 *Le Fourneau*, 1887. A corner of Seurat's studio on the Boulevard de Clichy. In the final picture the stove appears in the lower right-hand corner and the full-bellied form of the pot, or jug, forms a Vermeer-like note in a painting where a tender roundness recurs constantly.

respectively from the back, the front and the side. There are one or two incidental still-lifes. Seurat seems to have started from what must, in life, have been quite a deep recession: but in the finished picture his intention was clearly to establish a single, frieze-like plane in the foreground and to bring forward, immediately behind this, the remaining picture space in a shallow hoop-shape.

The motives behind the picture are manifold. To paint, in the first place, a divisionist nude, and to do it not once but three times, thus flouting those who said, or implied, that the new technique would not lend itself to this purpose. Next, to combine in those nudes the simplified linear patterns of Ingres with his own predilection for the figure seen as a flattened outline. Third (as Fénéon

180 *Une Poseuse Habillée, Buste de Profil, c.* 1887. Conceivably drawn from the same model, and in the same context, as *Ill. 145*

181 *Nature Morte (Chapeau et Parapluie) c.* 1887. The big hat and the umbrella, two favourite motifs with Seurat, may well have an emblematic meaning, now lost, in *Les Poseuses*

remarked in a text, dated April 1888, which the artist must have seen and approved), Seurat put into action certain of Charles Henry's theories: 'by a piece of pseudo-scientific fantasy, the red parasol, the straw-coloured parasol, and the green stocking are oriented in the directions adopted by red, yellow and green on Henry's chromatic circle'. Fourth, he aimed, for reasons that have never quite been fathomed, to play off the indoor nakedness of his living models

against the swathed outdoorness of the characters in his *Grande Jatte*. In the picture itself, as in the picture-within-the-picture, hats and parasols are strewn on the ground; the central nude stands on a mat or rug almost identical with those which, in the guise of reeds, or grasses, or patches of sunlight or shade, so persistently litter the foreground of Seurat's out-of-door pictures; and in the girl's discarded clothes there may well have been a social comment now lost to us,

182 (*left*) *La Poseuse de Profil*, 1887. In the final painting Seurat gave the model a much stronger definition, dispelled the wraiths of tone in which she is here floating, and gave her stockings—as much, no doubt, for the colour-note as for their appeal to his discreet but highly developed erotic sense. Mr Herbert points out that the pose here is that of 'the antique Spinario, or thorn-puller'

183 (*right*) *La Poseuse de Dos*, 1887. An instance of Seurat's determination, in the *Poseuses*, to achieve a depth and roundness of modelling which the dot had not hitherto yielded

184 *Petite Étude Complète pour Les Poseuses*, 1887. A very small (6 by 8 inches) but comprehensive working model for the final version. The vertical bands of colour at the edges gave place at a later stage to the frame, painted by Seurat himself to suit the picture, which so impressed Pissarro when he visited the studio in June 1887: 'It's indispensable', he wrote to Signac. 'We'll just have to do the same'

for Seurat was very sensitive to fashion, and to the equipment of urban life. On one level, *Les Poseuses* is a frontier raid into the academics' territory; on another it pays homage to the Ingres of *La Source* and *La Baigneuse de Valpinçon*; on a third, it is a technical manifesto, a *coup d'état* in regions which people had thought to be forbidden to him. But it is also a mysterious and original poetic conception, and it seems improbable that Seurat, of all people, should have included his *Grande Jatte* simply 'because it was there', or that, to mention one thing only, it should be by accident that the rounded and tender back of the nude on the left should blot out the symbolic monkey and its emblematic tail. To Félix Fénéon, who was never again to be so wholeheartedly enthusiastic about a painting by Seurat, the

185 (*right*) *Poseuse Debout, de Face*, 1886–7. An early oil-sketch, marked by vestigial criss-cross brushwork and a pose which, in the stance of the legs and feet, would never have kept the big final composition together

186 *Les Poseuses*, *Ensemble* (small version), oil on canvas (15½ by 19¼ inches), 1888

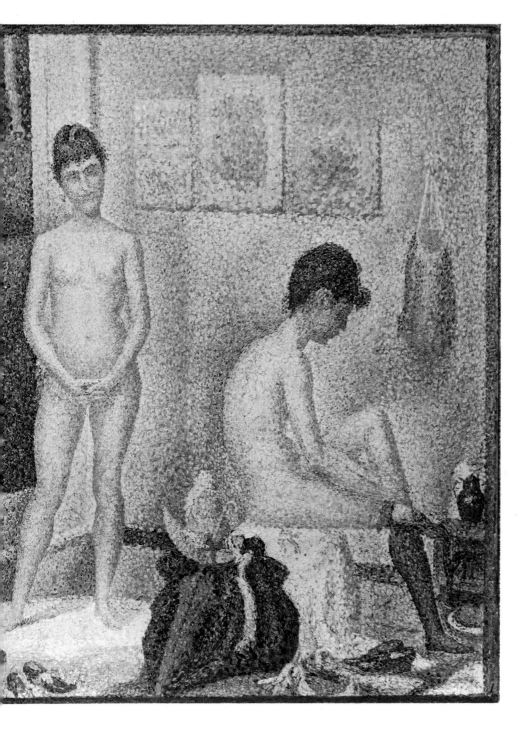

painting was an unqualified success: 'the ground-swell of a glorious and tranquil rhythm gives enhanced life to both colour and form,' he wrote, 'and *Les Poseuses* puts to shame the nudes that we see in art-galleries'.

Quite a few people—among them Van Gogh and Pissarro—came to see *Les Poseuses* at some stage in its progress; more and more painters, meanwhile, adopted the dot. This irritated Seurat, who wrote to Signac and said, 'The more numerous we are, the less original we shall be. The day will come when everyone will paint like us—and then our technique will be valueless and people will look for something else—as is happening already.' Seurat himself saw the dot merely as an expedient, and not a very satisfactory one, for producing an accurate *mélange optique*. In so far as the dot was concerned, he seems to have found *Les Poseuses* unsatisfactory, for hardly had he finished it than he began on a smaller version, less than one-sixth the size, in which the handling is noticeably more fluent and free (*Ill. 186*). This may have been partly due to difficulties he had with the canvas used for the *Poseuses*; Signac noted in August 1887 that the canvas caused the colours to change within forty-eight hours of their application. Or it may have been that, as Signac noted ten years later in his diaries, the strokes used had been so small as to make the procedure look petty and mechanical. Once again the paradox asserted itself that the technique which aimed at purity and saturation of colour ended by giving the whole picture a greyish, low-spirited look. And after *Les Poseuses* was finished and shown, at least one powerful nature had further doubts. 'I'm thinking very much', Pissarro wrote in September 1888, 'of how to do without the dot. I hope to succeed in it, but . . . how can one combine the purity and simplicity of the dot with the qualities of our Impressionism— the suppleness, the spontaneity, the freshness of sensation? That's the problem: and I'm always thinking of it, for the dot is thin, diaphanous, has no consistency, is more monotonous than simple— even with Seurat, above all with Seurat . . .'

To another great man, Seurat's significance lay elsewhere than in the dot. 'We can already foresee', Van Gogh wrote to his brother Théo, 'that this technique will not become a universal dogma more

187 *Les Poseuses*, autumn 1886 to spring 1888. 'One cannot move a button or a ribbon', Roger Fry wrote in 1926, 'without disaster to this amazingly complete and closely knit system. Since Poussin surely no one has been able to design in such elaborate and perfect counterpoint'

than any other.' And he forecasted, quite rightly, that 'Seurat's *Grande Jatte* will for that reason become in time even more personal and even more original'. Van Gogh had met Seurat in 1887 in the huge top-lit hall of a popular restaurant in the Avenue de Clichy, which Van Gogh had taken over, more or less, as an exhibition-gallery. Before long he acknowledged Seurat as the natural leader of those painters (himself, Gauguin, Toulouse-Lautrec and Emile Bernard) whom he described as 'le petit Boulevard', in contra-distinction to the old Impressionists. When he was in Arles he wrote to his brother of the big decorative scheme he had in progress and

188 *Clowns et Poney*, c. 1882–3. In its subject-matter this is near to *La Parade*, but Mr Herbert backdates it by four or five years on stylistic grounds; and it is true that Seurat here takes a more local and circumstantial view of the scene than was his custom in 1887–8. These could be identifiable clown in an identifiable setting, and not figures in Limbo, as in *La Parade*

189 *Clowns et Personnages*, c. 1887. The universalization of the figures, here, does not preclude some precise observation by Seurat: the clown's short and baggy trousers are, for instance, one of the classic uniforms of the circus

said, 'Tell Seurat that in this work on a larger scale I am often encouraged by the memory of his personality and of the visit we made to his studio to see his beautiful big canvases.' And of one of the most famous of his own pictures, the bedroom done at Arles, in October 1888, he later wrote to Gauguin that it was 'an interior of nothing at all, of a Seurat-like simplicity . . .'; and although he had long abandoned the dot, Van Gogh showed his loyalty to Seurat's ideas by pointing out that by the variety of vivid and pure colour in the picture he had aimed at 'an *absolute restfulness*—and there is no white in it at all except the little note produced by the mirror with its black frame (in order to get the fourth pair of complementaries into it).'

Van Gogh's visit to Seurat's studio was in February 1888, a time at which the 'beautiful big canvases' on view were presumably the *Baignade*, the *Grande Jatte*, the *Poseuses* and a large canvas much more recent in its origins: *La Parade de Cirque* (*Ill. 194*). Seurat seems to have painted this between the autumn of 1887 and the beginning of 1888; much more rapidly, therefore, than his earlier large pictures. It was the first product, on canvas, of an enthusiasm which had prompted him, during the winter of 1886–7, to make a whole corpus of marvellous drawings (*Ills. 188–92*). In his liking for the night-world of Paris Seurat fulfilled, to begin with, what was almost a local obligation, since his studio was in the middle of that world. But he obeyed, coincidentally, the imperative of the times, in that the mid-1880s were marked by a wave of infatuation among artists and poets with the circus, the café-concert, and their humbler derivatives. Not only

190 *Couple Dansant*, *c.* 1887. The image here is, as has often been said, like that of an Egyptian bas-relief; and the unheard music could be that which Shakespeare's Cleopatra first called for, in Act 2, scene V, and then on the instant countermanded

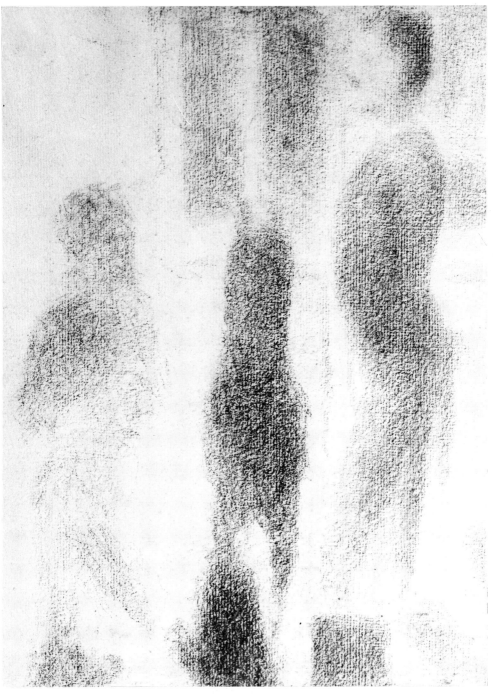

191 *Monsieur Loyal et Poney*, 1887. A drawing that has much to do with *La Parade*: the ringmaster, here, is the predominant figure, and the pony later gave place to the trombonist, but the frieze-like disposition of the flattened figures and the emblematic hats in the foreground are already beginning to assume their final attitudes

were many of the performers delightfully expert, but the performance itself had a fugitive, improvisatory quality, and an element
likewise of propitiation and sacrifice, which made it peculiarly
subject to poetic interpretation. The status of the performer—his
situation, that is to say, as both hero and martyr—had obvious
analogies with that of the poet and the artist. Seurat himself was free
from financial anxieties: but he must have known what others had
endured—how Pissarro, for one, in March 1887 had had to write
to his son and say: 'We live in an idiotic age, you know. Here am I,
who've done the work of four men to get some sort of honest
reputation, and what happens? I'm like a man singing in the street,
and when the song is over the bourgeois turns his back rather
than give me a penny for my trouble.' This is the parable which
Daumier, for one, had taken up in the wonderful series of *Parade*
drawings some twenty years earlier, and it seems improbable that
Seurat had not these in mind when he, in his turn, in 1887 or thereabouts took for the subject of one of his drawings a barker in the
gathering dusk.

His own *Parade* (*Ills. 193–4*) is now often discussed in terms of its
obedience to the theories of Charles Henry. Robert L. Herbert knows
of a document which proves beyond doubt that Seurat's architectural
background is based minutely upon the mathematical theories put
forward in 1885 in Henry's *Une Esthétique Scientifique*. He suggests,
further, that 'the expression of sad, calm and gay moods is linked with
downward, horizontal and upward linear directions as explained by
Henry's version of the pleasure–pain theory'. For the truth of this,
anyone who owns a ruler and a pair of compasses can vouch. The
picture also makes manifest Seurat's preoccupation with Egyptian
art, in the use of flattened, frieze-like silhouette. From his earlier
arboreal experiments there survives a single tree, hardly less eloquent
of desolation than the tree devised by Giacometti for *En Attendant
Godot*; and so that we should not doubt that the equivocal penumbra
is, in fact, that of gaslight, Seurat has added to the top of the composition an independent flat band on which are placed nine emblematic gas-lamps; the form of these lamps is that indicated by Seurat,
in a letter of 1890, as symbolical of festivity. From the rest of the

192 *Banquistes*, *c.* 1887. Midway between Daumier and Picasso, this drawing surpasses both of them in its unforced tenderness: once having seen it, we know for ever what it is like to wait to go on before a scanty and unappreciative audience

picture the note of festivity is, on the other hand, quite absent. The trombonist might be a headsman, and the subordinate musicians might be prisoners in the dock; the spectators would have as readily flocked to a public hanging; the bow-fronted Director is a monster of indifference and calculation. It is from the contrast between all this and the apparatus of festivity that the *Parade* derives its power to haunt. No amount of geometry can hide the fact that this picture offers a criticism of society.

But that criticism is a poet's, not a politician's. Seurat may have sympathized with his friends' political views (which were those of the extreme but independent Left) but he never defined his views in public, as Pissarro and Signac were to do after his death. It seems to me more profitable to look, for one of the origins of *La Parade de Cirque*, to Rimbaud's prose-poem *Parade* which had appeared on 13th May 1886 in *La Vogue*. The manuscript of Rimbaud's *Les Illuminations* had been edited by one close friend of Seurat's, Félix Fénéon, and published by another, Gustave Kahn. Seurat is known to have had the intellectual reviews of the day in his studio, and in view of his closeness to both Kahn and Fénéon it seems very unlikely indeed that he should not have read *Parade*. Not that the picture is in any way an 'illustration' of the prose-poem: simply that Seurat, like Rimbaud before him, held up the circuses of everyday as a mirror to the condition of mankind in the new-made industrial cities of the late nineteenth century. *Leur raillerie ou leur terreur dure une minute, ou des mois entiers*: and of all this Seurat, like Rimbaud, could say '*J'ai seul la clef de cette parade sauvage.*' Of how many of Seurat's metropolitan drawings could it not be said that they represent '*une métropole crue moderne parce que tout goût connu a été éludé dans les ameublements et l'extérieur des maisons aussi bien que dans le plan de la ville*'? His subject had always been, and was to be more than ever, '*ces millions de gens qui n'ont pas besoin de se connaître*'; and how often did he not see them as '*Des spectres . . . roulant à travers l'épaisse et éternelle fumée de charbon—notre ombre des bois, notre nuit d'été!*'? More than one of his early *croquetons* could carry an epigraph from Rimbaud's *Ouvriers*: '*La ville, avec sa fumée et ses bruits de métiers, nous suivant très loin dans les chemins. O l'autre monde, l'habitation bénie par*

193 *La Parade*, 1887. Save for the tree on the left, and for some marks of inattention among the audience, this tiny (barely 5 by 8 inches) pen-drawing has the essential of the finished painting, and it shows, coincidentally, how close in this instance were Seurat's graphic procedures to his technique in oils.

le ciel et les ombrages!' More than once, likewise, Seurat's handling of Parisian canalscape has its parallel in Rimbaud: *'Des ciels gris de cristal. Un bizarre dessin de ponts, ceux-ci droits, ceux-là bombés, d'autres descendant ou obliquant en angles sur les premiers, et ces figures se renouvelant dans les autres circuits éclairés du canal, mais tous tellement longs et legers que les rives, chargées de dômes s'abaissent et s'amoindrissent.'*

In dealing with metropolitan life, Seurat reveals himself as a poet, and as a moralist, and as a critic of society. (Much could be said in this context of the *Tour Eiffel* of 1889. In this tiny painting, *Ill. 173*, Seurat identified himself with a triumph of the modern spirit— Eiffel himself had likened it to the pyramids—which at that time was painted with newly-invented pigments that gave it a startling and iridescent appearance. Actually to like the Eiffel Tower at that time was to alienate all those who cared for conventional 'fine taste').

194 *La Parade de Cirque*, 1887–8. Last seen in London in 1932, this great picture now reigns over the French nineteenth-century rooms in the Metropolitan Museum, New York, as *Une Baignade, Asnières* reigns over the equivalent rooms in the National Gallery

He also affected, time and again, the preoccupations of his friends. What he said to them, we shall never know: but as he had the strongest and most consistent head among them we can reasonably infer that he had a good deal to do with the opinions that they expressed afterwards. When Signac wrote in his diary that 'Divisionism is a philosophy, not a system', it really meant something. Divisionism was more than a way of painting pictures. When Signac saw some ugly houses, in September 1894, he wrote in his diary: 'It made me want to publish the little instrument—a chromatic circle and a screen —that specifies the two, three or four colours that go well together in any particular case. It would be invaluable to dressmakers, house-painters, and carpet-designers, and would save them from the big mistakes which too often ruin their finest creations. A little printed note would explain to them that if they have, say, a red and want to find two other colours that will go well with it they have only to turn the circle to find the best possible combination.' Somewhere in all this there was probably a reminiscence of Seurat's conversation— or an inference from it.

Arbitrary as the *Parade* may be in many of its elements, and set as Seurat was on adjusting the visible world to suit the schema of his *grandes machines*, he was as strict as ever about the observances owed to nature in his landscapes. In Honfleur, he had left the Kröller-Müller *Coin d'un Bassin* unfinished rather than fake it up after the ships had sailed, and when he went to Port-en-Bessin in the summer of 1888 he kept as carefully as any beginner to the given detail of the scene. But, although there was no question of his forcing nature to his own ends, it remained open to him to choose the motifs which best suited those ends, and to garnish them with equivocal incident.

In the Minneapolis *Pont et les Quais à Port-en-Bessin* (*Ill. 196*), for instance, the long descending line of the cliffs from left to right has its counterpart in earlier paintings from Grandcamp and Honfleur. But whereas in earlier summers Seurat would walk long distances to find motifs that for some reason suited him, at Port-en-Bessin he seems to have decided to make an inventory of the little harbour, surveying it in detail from four different angles in the paintings now

195 *L'Avant-port à Port-en-Bessin, Marée Haute*, oil on canvas, 1888

at, respectively, Minneapolis (*Ill. 196*), St Louis (*Ill. 197*), the Louvre (*Ill. 195*) and the Kröller-Müller Museum, Otterlo (*Ill. 200*). This harbour gave him the enclosed, interlocking, sharp-angled forms that he delighted in: it gave him bridges, sails, quaysides, weird specimens of seaside architecture, masts, lamp-posts, a jagged descending line of cliffs and a serpentine path. Sometimes, as in the St Louis picture (*Ill. 197*), the flat forms of jetty and quayside are disposed like the raised areas in one of Ben Nicholson's recent reliefs, and the town itself reverts to the frieze-like structure of Seurat's figure subjects. These are some of the most marvellously constructed of all Seurat's paintings, and there is an ideal dignity in his handling

196 *Le Pont et les Quais à Port-en-Bessin*, oil on canvas, 1888

of the early ironwork structures (notably in the Minneapolis picture, *Ill. 196*), where the notion of the music of space comes out strongly. All this can be seen as a development, natural in one so systematic, from the earlier *marines*: but what is new in the Port-en-Bessin pictures is the use of symbolic arabesque. In the Louvre picture, *Ill. 195* (whose construction, by the way, is that of the *Bec du Hoc*, *Ill. 159*, reversed and laid on its side), the cliff path is given by nature: but it is the ancestor, all the same, of that extraordinary passage in *Le Circue* (*Ill. 225*) where the ringmaster's whip lies coiled on the floor and the clown's long streamer passes out of the picture altogether, reappearing higher up like a disconnected lightning-flash.

More remarkable still is the behaviour of the flags in the Kröller-Müller picture (*Ill. 200*). These are agitated by what is surely the only high wind in all Seurat, and their festive tonality contrasts completely with the rather low-spirited gamut of the rest of the picture. Their relation to the clouds is to be found not in nature, but rather in some diagrammatic language of the emotions: and in *Le Chahut* (*Ill. 207*), which is this picture's neighbour in the Kröller-Müller Museum, the forked and sinuous outline of the topmost flag recurs almost identically in the flying coat-tails of the male dancer. Seurat was the last painter in the world not to notice such a similarity: there was in both cases a declaration of high spirits, however ironically those high spirits might be commented upon elsewhere in the picture.

197 *L'Avant-port à Port-en-Bessin*, oil on canvas, 1888

In the Harriman *Les Grues et La Percée, Port-en-Bessin* (*Ill. 199*), the emblematic use of natural forms recurs markedly in Seurat's cloud-structures; and in the Museum of Modern Art's *Entrée de l'Avant-Port* (*Ill. 198*) the Port-en-Bessin series reaches an even greater degree of sophistication in the extraordinarily subtle and arguably quite unrealistic submission of natural fact to a constructive scheme which combines several of Seurat's favourite motifs: the elongated ovals of the rug-shapes (in this case the reflections cast on the sea by low cloud), the open angles and shallow curves of sailing-boats on the move, the long, echoing curve of the path on shore, and the horizon, pitched even higher than in *Le Bec du Hoc*, which suggests that, as in his early *croquetons*, Seurat had decided to cut off the upper part of his field of vision.

Only once did Seurat attempt an inhabited coast-scape. Neither at Le Crotoy in 1889 nor at Gravelines in 1890 did he people the grave and tranquil canvases; these could indeed be said to relate to a world too perfect in its equilibrium to tolerate human disturbance. But in the Minneapolis *Le Pont et Les Quais, Port-en-Bessin* (*Ill. 196*) the three figures in the foreground have been interpreted not as animated bollards or convenient space-markers, but as the instruments of social comment. William I. Homer has contrasted 'the dejected cast of the two middle-class working people [*sic*]' with the child which 'gives the scene a hopeful cast because of its alert glance and air of self-contained energy. This may have been the image that symbolized for Seurat, unconsciously, the new artistic and social generation to which he belonged.' It is true, admittedly, that these three figures are more firmly defined, in their social context, than those in any other of Seurat's sea-coast pictures; but at the same time, the bowler-hatted man could be said to come from stock (his double appears in the Courtauld *Pont de Courbevoie*—*Ill. 201*—and as Fénéon noted in 1889, he is also very near to the Director in *La Parade de Cirque*); and the little boy is Seurat's standard frontal image of early youth. Perhaps the answer is simply that Seurat was not quite sure how far he could go, or ought to go, with the figures: whether he should subordinate them completely to the abstract forms of his landscape, or whether he could, on the contrary, allow

198 *Entrée de l'Avant-Port à Port-en-Bessin*, oil on canvas, 1888

them their full liberty as individual human beings and members of a defined social group. (He it was, after all, who said—my italics—'I want to make modern people move about as if they were on the Parthenon frieze *in their most essential characteristics*.') Had he made more pictures of this sort, he would certainly have settled the problem: as it was, he alternated for the rest of his life between indoor figure-subjects and landscapes to which the human race was not allowed entrance.

The paintings done at Port-en-Bessin in the summer of 1888 are among the most complex, and the most completely realized, in all

227

Seurat's output. In the Harriman *Les Grues et La Percée, Port-en-Bessin* (*Ill. 199*) he comes as near as he ever came in painting to the rhetoric of nature: but even there the curious mast-like structure in the top left corner of the canvas reassures us that the whole organization is under control, and this impression is confirmed when we note that the border of the canvas has also been painted by Seurat: Art here has the upper hand.

This device of painting the border, or in certain cases the frame, was one of the ideas with which Seurat had occupied himself in the years immediately after the *Grande Jatte*. He had abandoned the classic gold frame, on the grounds that it destroyed any orangey tones in his paintings, and he was not happy with the Impressionists'

199 *Les Grues et La Percée à Port-en-Bessin*, oil on canvas, 1888

200 *Dimanche, Port-en-Bessin*, oil on canvas, 1888

plain white frame, since this set up too abrupt a contrast with the painting. Already with the *Grande Jatte* he had painted a narrow border on the canvas itself: a border of complementaries which helped the observer to adjust between the canvas and the surrounding wall (*Ill. 133*). But this was only one of the problems which taxed him, and made him more than usually secretive and irritable, after the summer of 1886. His Belgian friends and admirers had told him frankly, when the *Grande Jatte* was shown in Brussels in the winter of 1886–7, that they did not think that it worked properly from a distance; and he had found that the scientific exactitude of the colour-relations within the picture was falsified within a few weeks of its

229

completion by the fact that some colours held fast and others did not. (Fénéon was to write in 1892 that 'the *Grande Jatte* has lost its luminous charm: the reds and blues have held firm, but the Veronese greens have turned olive-green, and the orange tones which represented light are now nothing but holes'.

This difficult period was first elucidated in its biographical detail by Professor Rewald, and from the documents he has published it is clear that Seurat was under great nervous strain while working on *Les Poseuses*. 'I don't understand anything any more,' he wrote to Signac in August 1887, 'work is difficult, and I am seeing nobody.' There were two reasons for this heightened solitude. One was that, as Verhaeren said later, Seurat never regarded his friends and colleagues as being anywhere near as good as he was; the other, that he was obsessed with the fear that other people would get hold of his ideas, adapt them wrongly or superficially, and in general interfere with the ordered evolution of his gifts. All his friends knew of this, and most of them respected his feelings. After Pissarro, for instance, had seen the painted frame for *Les Poseuses* he wrote to Signac that it was obviously the only solution: 'The picture is not at all the same picture if it has white (or anything else) all round it. I shall try it myself—but of course I shall only exhibit the result after Seurat has made it known that he thought of it first.'

Meanwhile the original small band of neo-impressionists had been joined by others, both in Paris and in Brussels. Some of these were really no good at all and had quite failed to heed, or perhaps had not read, Fénéon's original warning: that 'if Monsieur X were to study treatises on optics for all eternity he could never paint the *Grande Jatte*....The method demands an exceptionally delicate eye, and ... is accessible only to *painters*.' Between those who, like Dubois-Pillet, went conscientiously into the findings of people like the early-nineteenth-century English theorist Thomas Young, and those who simply took over the dot and hoped for the best, a great gap yawned; but Seurat saw them one and all as one vast collective nuisance, and there is no doubt that he was delighted to get away from Paris and work in peace at the seaside. Of this, the masterpieces produced at Port-en-Bessin (*Ills. 195–200*) are evidence.

His stay there was not, even so, without incident. In August 1888 Arsène Alexandre published an account of the neo-impressionist movement in which he said that 'ill-informed critics or unscrupulous colleagues' had 'all but deprived Seurat of the paternity of his theory'. The squabble which resulted is of interest: first, because it forced Seurat for once to reveal himself a little in writing and, second, because it prompted even Pissarro, that noblest of natures, to express feelings which normally he would have been too magnanimous to set down on paper.

When Signac asked Seurat to tell him frankly if he had leaked his feelings to Arsène Alexandre, Seurat replied that he had not seen the article, and that as far as Alexandre was concerned he had simply said what he had always thought: that the auxiliary divisionists were an encumbrance and could only do harm to the truly gifted members of the group, and that he himself had adopted divisionism to make it possible for him to realize his own nature in paint, and for no other reason. He had seen Alexandre more than a year before (that is, in the summer of 1887): and to make things doubly clear he added, on a separate piece of paper, the words: 'I have never called anyone an "unscrupulous colleague", and I still consider Fénéon's pamphlet as the expression of my ideas about painting.'

'I never say much, anyway' was another of his reactions to Signac's letter. But he must have said enough to cause misgivings, for when Pissarro learned of the incident he wrote to Signac that: 'It's disquieting. For the future of our "impressionist" art we must absolutely stay outside the influence of the School of Seurat. (You yourself saw this coming, by the way.) *Seurat is a graduate of the Ecole des Beaux-Arts*, and he's absolutely soaked in it. So look out! That way danger lies. This is not a question of technique or science, but of a tradition which must be kept intact. Science belongs to everyone, and you must use it if you want to, but hold tight to the gift which you have: that of feeling as a free and independent artist. Leave Seurat to work out his problems. They will have their usefulness, I don't doubt, and anyway that's what he's there for.'

All this was a summer storm, at most, and when Seurat got back to Paris he began to think of how best to adapt to metropolitan life

201 *Le Pont de Courbevoie*, 1886–7, oil on canvas, 18 by 21 inches. One of the most tightly constructed of all Seurat's landscapes, this is a kind of *summa* of his metropolitan practice. Everything tells: the tree on the right, bent near its base like a human elbow; the standard Seurat manikins at the water's edge; the interlocked verticals and horizontals that work equally well on the picture-surface and as indicators of recession; the fuzz of foliage that answers to the lapsed diagonal of the riverbank; the contrasting outline of the sail; and the pure rectangles that offset the improvisatory untidiness of nature

the flat curvilinear arabesques, precursors of the *Jugendstil*, which had made their appearance in his Port-en-Bessin land- and sea-scapes. It was characteristic of his deliberate nature that he was able to swing at will from an almost uninhabited natural scene to the frantic agitations of a big city. And he saw those agitations in a way that was literally up-to-the-minute: through the posters of Jules Chéret, which were turning the boulevards into an unacknowledged art-gallery. Not long after Seurat died, an article appeared in *La Plume* to the effect that what suited one kind of art would not suit another. 'You can't imagine', the author said, 'an illuminated manuscript on canvas . . . or, for that matter, a Chéret turned fresco.' But 'a Chéret turned fresco' is precisely what Seurat was after in two of his last canvases: *Le Chahut* (*Ill. 207*) and *Le Cirque* (*Ill. 225*). He had long admired Chéret's posters (one of which hung in his studio in the Passage de l'Elysée des Beaux-Arts) and, like many other artists, he regarded Chéret's work as a cut above commercial art. Degas and Forain thought much of him; he was singled out by Huysmans; he showed in Brussels with Seurat, Pissarro and Sisley; he appeared alongside Whistler and Redon in the *Revue Indépendante*; in 1890 a critic noted that in his latest posters the laws of contrasts and complementaries were carefully observed. (Those who know Chéret's paintings will have noticed in some of them a blonde tonality not unlike that of Seurat's *Cirque*.) Chéret's contemporaries likened him to Tiepolo mainly, one must assume, because both had a great taste for anti-gravitational subjects: what Seurat prized in Chéret was, rather, the nice adaptation of his gifts to subjects that were literally up-to-the-minute. This admiration was common form in Seurat's circle. Ten years after Seurat's death, for instance, his friend Gustave Kahn published a book called *L'Esthétique de la Rue*, in which he praises Chéret in terms that could as well be applied to Seurat: Chéret's poster for Loïe Fuller, for instance, brought off to admiration the almost impossible task of suggesting that the dancer's vertiginous movement had been caught in full career; and in the *Coulisses de l'Opéra* for the Musee Grévin Chéret had so placed his tall hieratic forms that the observer had the sensation of looking in 'through a momentarily opened door at a scene blazing with

202 (*right*) *Scène de Théâtre, c.* 1887–8. This is a particular moment in a particular play, worked up on a considerable scale (12 by 16 inches) and with the audience kept down below the sight-line of the observer

203 *La Loge de l'Artiste*, *c.* 1887. In its casual, snapshot-like composition this back-stage scene may owe something to Degas, with whose night-subjects of a decade earlier Seurat was certainly familiar

unaccustomed light'. And, of course, artificial light had at that time connotations of hectic excitement. Its pristine associations with fairy-land had given place to affinities altogether more rowdy; and Kahn looked forward to the time when a perfected society would do away with advertising, and the garish illuminated sign would be replaced by the play of coloured lights (chosen, doubtless, according to divisionist principles).

What Seurat wanted to do, meanwhile, was to touch the nerve of modern life, as Chéret did, and at the same time to strike the universal note which he had learned from Charles Henry. If he managed to do both these things he would have extended still further the range of his art and got clear of his own followers, some of whom were beginning to affect him as much as certain insects affected the Victorian equatorial explorer.

204 *A la Gaité-Rochechouart*, 1887–8. One of the many drawings of the period 1887–8 in which Seurat took the scene as it actually presented itself: only later, when working up *Le Chahut*, did he select and simplify and embellish and recompose

205 *Au Concert Européen*, 1887–8. Probably the most masterly of all Seurat's café-concert drawings, and one in which he makes marvellous play with the undulating line made by the chairbacks, by the shoulders of the spectators, their hats, and by the singer's upraised arms

206 *High C*, 1887–8. The hat on the extreme left, the singer's right arm, even the movement of the spectators' heads from left to right—all are so many emblems of steepness, and persuade us almost that we can hear the top note in question

Seurat's first direct adaptation of Chéret occurred when, in 1889, he made a cover-design for a novel called *La Ménagerie Sociale*. This had been written under the pseudonym of Victor Jozé by Victor Dobrski, who had been active in propagandizing for the neo-impressionists in Poland. As Robert L. Herbert has pointed out, it is very close to a poster for *L'Amant des Danseuses* which Chéret had produced the previous year. Seurat took over from Chéret not only the composition and the stance and dress of the male figure, but also the rather primitive signals with which Chéret indicated the disposition and state of mind of his characters. Soon afterwards the word got about that Seurat was aiming to paint a large picture in which the principles, and the apparatuses, of Charles Henry would be allied to the subject-matter and the stylistic approach of Chéret: this was *Le Chahut* (*Ill. 207*), which was first shown at the Salon des Indépendants in March 1890.

Le Chahut was built up in part from material noted down *sur le motif* at the time when Seurat lived much in the Parisian night-world. The left side of the canvas draws heavily, for instance, on his *Le Divan Japonais* (Cdh 690); the conductor's profile appears in the Fogg Art Museum *A la Gaité-Rochechouart* (*Ill. 204*), and the form of the double bass and sheet music in the Van Gogh *Chanteuse au Café-Concert* (Cdh 688). These were themes that Seurat kept in mind for two, possibly for three, years before setting to work. The result has nothing of the velvety softness and smoothness and the apparent informality of the drawings, in which the white forms are laid like camellia-petals on some of Seurat's subtlest and most delicately organized gradations. We have in their stead a characteristic mingling of details minutely observed with clusters or aggregates of emblematic forms. Nowhere does Seurat scrutinize more closely the apparatus of modernity than in the light-fittings to the left, or the tailoring of the bassist's coat, or the hat and cane of the spectator in the lower right corner. But no sooner are these taken in than we note the profusion of references which could have been devised by Charles Henry himself as illustrations to one of his Sorbonne lectures: the relation between the male dancer's coat-tails and the women's shoulder-ornaments, for instance, or between his moustaches and her

207 *Le Chahut*, oil on canvas (67 by 55 inches). For all the determined gaiety of its components, a certain rusty and claustrophobic sadness is the mark of this painting

lips, or between the bows of the women's shoes and the conductor's moustache and the upper of the two light-fittings on the left. We notice that the forms of the sheet music are those of the white sails in Seurat's *marines*; that even the white lining of the male dancer's hat plays its part in the articulation of the design; and that in painting the conductor and the bassist Seurat has assimilated the colour of their hair to the colour of the cloth of their coats. Spatially this is one of his most cryptic paintings: it is as if he had taken the subject and wrapped it round an invisible central axis. In its shallow picture-space and determination to give us more of the scene than could be glimpsed from any point, Seurat here anticipates Cubist practice, and it may not be without significance that Braque in 1907 had a reproduction of this picture pinned up in his studio.

Of the picture's diagrammatic qualities, use of the golden section and reliance on a Henryesque schema of upward-flying lines, much has been written. Seurat achieved by all this an incorporeal effect, a denial of weight and effort which could be said to be appropriate to the subject. (Chéret, in November 1888, had done precisely this: Fénéon wrote of his poster for *L'Echo de Paris* that it had 'an intoxica-tion of high spirits that never leads to grimaces; bodies bend low and leap into the air with never an ugly movement; dizzy and delightful are the arms and legs that shoot out from the high-kicking group. M. Chéret's style may once have been blatant and showy; today it has lost all its fat and has a lyrical, radiant purity . . .') But not everyone, even among Seurat's admirers, loved the picture; one of them wrote in August 1890 that 'Chéret's marvellous posters are a thousand times more expressive, in colour and in design, than *Le Chahut*.' (Mr Aaron Scharf has suggested, convincingly to my mind, that in the images of motion in *Le Chahut* Seurat was influ-enced by the serial-photography of Marey, which he could well have studied at the time.)

Fénéon never wrote on any of Seurat's last three major paintings, and already in September 1889 there was a note of caution in his article on the fifth exhibition of the Indépendants. 'M. Seurat knows very well', Fénéon wrote, 'that a line has an abstract significance (and one which can be evaluated) quite independent of its role in

208 (*right*) *Le Danseur à la Canne*, c. 1889–90. A late drawing that has just the fugacity, the unforced and festive lightness, that *Le Chahut* nowhere achieves

topography. In each of his landscapes the forms are governed by one or two basic directions. These directions are paired off with the picture's dominant colours, and any accessory lines are made to contrast with the picture's governing directions. Notice in the *Le Crotoy, Après-Midi*, the strip of sand which comes up from the lower left corner towards the littoral, and the cloud, shaped like a mushroom or a jelly-fish, which drops its vertical filaments towards the horizon line. These are contrasts of precisely the kind that M. Chéret uses so freely. Perhaps it is they which make his posters so effective. Such is the instinctive candour of M. Seurat's art that it never occurs to him to conceal his researches: we are the less ready, therefore, to believe in the spectacle that he puts before us.' And still today, seventy and more years later, there is an implausibility in these late subject-pictures which pulls many enthusiasts up short— and it is the more remarkable when we remember the marvellously easy and natural look of the drawings from which part of their material was drawn.

'Implausible' is not quite the word for the other major novelty which Seurat put on view in March 1890. The *Jeune Femme se Poudrant* (*Ill. 209*) has, on the contrary, turned with the years into a veritable icon of bourgeois correctitude. Not only is the rendering of the pseudo-rustic folding wall-mirror, the mass-produced *table de toilette* and the would-be elegant apparatus of beauty almost comical in its completeness, but the impeccable podge is herself a museum-piece. Everything about her, from the soft rounded fullness of her forms to the diminutive earrings and the broad flat armlet, is as true and right in its social definition as is the 'placing' of Chérie in the Goncourts' novel. But this is, for all that, one of Seurat's most mysterious pictures. It would be difficult, for instance, to say from what quarter the light is falling, or from what presumptions Seurat derived what Roger Fry called the 'theoretical and abstract colouring', or what is the intention behind the butterfly-shaped decoration immediately above the table mirror. Henri Dorra has suggested that, once again, Seurat used the golden section and that, characteristically, he put the exact centre of the neckline of the dress at the intersection of the golden section and the central

209 *Jeune Femme se Poudrant*, oil on canvas (37½ by 31¼ inches), 1890

210 *Femme Nue Étendue, c.* 1888. The only late drawing of the nude by Seurat that is known to have survived. Very possible Madeleine Knobloch, his mistress, was the model

horizontal axis of the picture; and Seurat was doubtless well aware of the ironical contrast between the restrained and portly sitter and the fever of excitement with which he must have gone about his discreet and elaborate designs.

Where so much is arbitrary and enigmatical, one thing can be suggested with confidence: that in his choice of motif for the wall, Seurat consciously picked on the formula which, in August 1890, he defined as the linear symbol of gaiety: $\underline{V}$. For the sitter was his mistress, Madeleine Knobloch: and in February 1890, if Signac's dating is correct, she had a son by him. Conceivably, therefore, the conundrums of the *Jeune Femme se Poudrant* are, in fact, so many emblems of felicity.

A. PAUL ALEXIS   SEURAT

211 *Paul Alexis*, 1888. Alexis had written on Seurat since 1884. A lively and prolific journalist and friend of Cézanne and Zola, he was one of those who in the 1880s kept open the lines of communication between art and literature

212 *Étude pour 'Le Cirque'*, 1890. At rather less than a third of full-size, this working-sketch blocked in the main compositional outlines of the final picture

CHAPTER SIX

A Career Cut Short

During the last summer of his life, Seurat went to Gravelines. (His stay at Le Crotoy, the previous year, had been cut short by the news of Madeleine Knobloch's pregnancy.) To have some idea of the incongruity (in the context of the accepted art of the day) of the pictures which resulted, one must recall that at the Salon of 1889 the great successes were Carolus-Duran's *Triumph of Bacchus*, Bonnat's *Enfin Seuls*, and Dagnan-Bouveret's *Pardon*. In the mixed shows of the late 1880s the visitor could expect, according to Gustave Kahn, to find 'some magnificent men-at-arms, the traditional huntsman on foot, the statutory *Corner of the Halles*, the eternal Joan of Arc, a Lady Macbeth, an assortment of Salomes, Jobs, Judiths, and St John the Baptists, some smithy scenes of course, some Spanish mandolinists, a few oriental monarchs from olden times, bituminous cuts from humble life and some likenesses of society women, served up swimming in cream'.

Such was the majority taste of the generation which saw produced in the summer of 1890 four of the most beautiful coast-scapes in European art. None was more than three feet across, with the result that Seurat never had to broaden or to enlarge his touch: all was measured, unemphatic and serene. His subject was the canal of Gravelines and the point where it is about to join the sea. There exist four pencil-studies of ships, masts, anchors and the far bank, and four oil-studies, of which one, formerly owned by Maximilian Luce, comes quite close to the Indianapolis *Le Chenal de Gravelines, Petit Fort-Philippe* (*Ill. 217*) and another, now in St Tropez (*Ill. 214*), foreshadows the *Le Chenal de Gravelines, Un Soir* (*Ill. 215*). Much can be learnt from both; in the sketches Seurat employs the clotted, more obviously 'painterly' approach of his earlier oil-sketches, with each touch clearly visible and a physical richness and liveness both in the

213 *Arbres et Bateaux*, 1890. While at Gravelines Seurat made a number of independent oil-panel studies in pure divisionist style. Like the one here, they were the same size as the many little panels with which, eight years earlier, he had begun his career as an independent painter

structure of the paint and in the grasp of the broad outline of the scene (*Ills. 213, 214*). When he came to the final painting (*Ill. 215*) there was in both cases a withdrawal from this first position. Nature's own accents were disallowed, the light became everywhere gentle and diffused, space-markers were laid out with an oriental delicacy, and for the rough dramas of everyday Seurat substituted an equilibrium of wraiths and spectres, a pale wonderland more haunting than the sumptuous imaginings of a Monticelli or even of a Gustave Moreau.

More precisely, Seurat laid in anchors where he needed them, much as Hokusai laid in a scaffolding in front of Fujiyama. Where the line on the canal bank, in the Indianapolis picture, was almost straight in the sketch (*Ill. 216*), for the final picture (*Ill. 217*) Seurat moved his viewpoint several feet to the left, so that he got a contrasting curve; and whereas in the sketch a ship lay in the left foreground and, by implication, narrowed the space from one bank to the other, Seurat later pushed it across to the far side and put one of his most redoubtable bollards on the near side of the parapet. With the anchors in the one picture (*Ill. 215*), and the bollard in the other (*Ill. 217*), he introduced at one stroke an element at once ordered and august.

On all four of the Gravelines pictures Seurat painted a dark border that contains and emphasizes the idiosyncratic pallor of the scene within; Wagnerian as were his sympathies and those of his friends (Charles Henry once wrote a prose-poem called 'Vision' in which he hears, at the end, the last scene of 'Meistersinger'), it is rather of Debussy that we think when, near the right-hand edge of *Ill. 222*, Seurat touches in the cylindrical bollard without which, we at once realize, the picture would not make sense at all. Banished from the Gravelines pictures are those points of ambiguity and disturbance which marked the coast-scenes of earlier years: the heavily symbolic clouds, the commotions of wind and weather, the massive opposition of cliffs and flat water and the rare forays into social comment.

214 *Étude pour 'Gravelines, Un Soir'*, 1890. Seurat was to make radical changes in this composition before he enlarged it: and, quite apart from this, the fat, separable strokes of the little sketch gave way to a delicate all-over speckle (see *Ill. 215*)

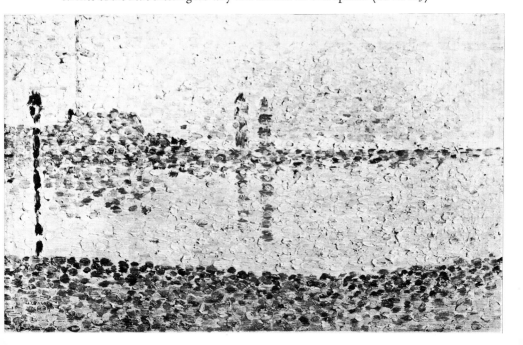

215 *Chenal de Gravelines: Un Soir*, oil on canvas, 1890. Seurat was always drawn to the enclosed forms of harbour and canal, and to the items of marine furniture which gave an epigrammatic finality to compositions thought out to their smallest detail: this painting contrasts absolutely, for instance, with those passages in *Le Chahut* where physical energy is made palpable

Nothing is here but the music of the eye: the Gravelines pictures are no more 'about' a named harbour than Stubbs' *Hambledonian Rubbing Down* is 'about' the training of thoroughbreds. In so far as these Gravelines pictures are about anything, in that sense, they are about man's capacity to master himself and his environment: about his power to collect, classify, analyse and redistribute the evidence of his senses: and about the application to these problems of the classic French qualities of lucidity, perseverance, and organization. Seurat does not need to strike an attitude in all this: we know, without his telling us, that a whole man has been at work in these canvases, and that their style results not from slavish devotion to a given set of rules but rather from the rarest and most perfect alliance of poetic sensibility with complete technical assurance.

Not that assurance was infallible: from the way in which the outline of the far bank can be seen through the pink sails of the incoming ship in the Kröller-Müller *Le Chenal de Gravelines, Direction de la Mer* (*Ill. 218*) it would seem that this ship was put in as an afterthought. But, as against this, Seurat was able in this series of paintings to carry perfect conviction with just the kind of visual puns and *correspondances* which, in his Parisian night-pieces, fell short of plausibility. In that same *Gravelines, Direction de la Mer*, where even the inexpressiveness of the title is significant, there are points at which cross calls to cross, or a group of verticals signals to its neighbour, and the eye takes in the affinities of form before the brain has had time to give those forms a name. At such moments the picture seems to take over, as an autonomous object, from the record of observable fact—and, in so doing, jumps forward not merely to the Kandinsky of the 1920s but to the art of the 1950s and 1960s.

When Seurat got back to Paris from Gravelines he began work on the picture which, in the event, was his last: *Le Cirque* (*Ill. 225*). At this time the circus in Paris was, like the café-concert, a favourite resort of painters and writers. It took place not in the gigantic rings or arenas of Anglo-Saxon or German derivation, but in buildings small enough for every wink to carry to the seats that rose steeply from the very edge of the *piste*. (Seurat, like Degas and Toulouse-Lautrec, was particularly inspired by the Cirque Fernando, later

216 *Petit Fort-Philippe*, 1890. For once in Seurat's work, this Conté crayon drawing establishes a deep recession to a horizon laid out in terms of classical Renaissance perspective: the soft tonality, which avoids both extremes of the black-and-white gamut, is characteristic of the Gravelines drawings

called the Cirque Médrano and only recently closed.) It was an intimate art, and one in which the public, almost as much as the performers, was on show. As an architectural subject for Seurat, the circus was ideal. It had verticals and horizontals as clearly defined as those of the harbour's edge; it had the contrasting curve of curtain and circular *piste*; and instead of imposing upon the scene the whip-lash arabesque he had learned from Chéret, the painter found a real-life whiplash already in position. The mood of euphoria, real or simulated, was so nearly universal as to demand the application of Supervillean principles to such physiognomies as needed to be deciphered; and the lighting and colour-range had an extravagant, metallic, artificial and apparently arbitrary character which was also perfectly in keeping with Seurat's practice at this time.

Le Cirque was never quite finished. (The severe geometrical framework on which Seurat was basing it can still be glimpsed at many points.) So dominant was Seurat's interest in surface-pattern at this stage that horse, rider and acrobat are not at all fixed, in conventional terms, in relation to their surroundings and could almost be paper cut-outs. The public appears mostly as a snouted gang of near-Mongolian extraction; there is some attempt to establish their social standing in inverse ratio to the level of their seats, but the best we can say is that Seurat, in this instance, was no

217 *Le Chenal de Gravelines: Petit Fort-Philippe*, 1890. A glance back at *Ill. 216* will show with what enormous and thorough-minded subtlety Seurat re-composed the initial idea for this very beautiful painting

218 *Le Chenal de Gravelines: Direction de la Mer*, 1890. The masts on the right have the role which was deputed, in *Ill. 215*, to the up-ended anchors. The hull-forms look back to the little panels done at Grandcamp in 1885, and the lighthouse and its auxiliaries to the factories in *Une Baignade, Asnières*. But the organization of all this in the curious rhomboid space is signed and dated 'Gravelines, 1890'

Daumier. As Robert L. Herbert has pointed out, the rider and the acrobatic clown derive directly from identifiable posters by Chéret, and it is also from Chéret that Seurat drew the high thin colour-gamut. But there are also many things to indicate that Seurat himself has been on hand: the baton held by the clown in the foreground, for instance, which closes the lower left corner of the composition exactly as do the flute in *Le Chahut* (*Ill. 207*) and the raft in *Le Chenal de Gravelines, Direction de la Mer* (*Ill. 218*).

219 *Régates à la Grenouillière*, Conté crayon drawing, 1890. Both Monet and Renoir had painted, twenty-one years earlier, this favourite bathing-place on the Seine near Bougival

Of the trend of feeling in Seurat's circle, nothing is more indicative than Signac's portrait of Félix Fénéon. Painted in 1890, this shows the critic, cyclamen in hand, against a background of formalized arabesques, some of them almost identical with certain favourites of Seurat's, and all of them decipherable according to the latest publications of Charles Henry: the *Cercle Chromatique*, the *Rapporteur Esthétique*, and the *Education du sens des formes*. In the *Cercle Chromatique*, published in 1888, Henry said, among much else, that angles of 30 and 60 degrees to the horizontal are *dynamogènes*: and, as Dorra has calculated, these angles recur at more than one crucial point in *Le Cirque*.

There are also said to be in existence documentary proofs of other, and more abstruse, mathematical intentions of Seurat, while his reliance on the golden section is never in doubt. Not only is it a golden section which marks off one world from the other (the artists' entrance, that is to say, from the tiered seats), but the rider's foot rests precisely on the vertical line of yet another golden section. The height of the picture, again, is twice the length of the golden section of its width. The colour-gamut corresponds to the colour circle devised by Henry. As in Cubist painting, the rearground is not allowed to recede, as would happen in Renaissance painting, but is raised and tipped forward to form a shallow picture-space.

220 *La Voile Blanche*, Conté crayon drawing, 1890. What turned out to be Seurat's last group of independent drawings had to do, as here, with that favourite motif of his: the white sail in the middle distance

221 *Le Crotoy, Aval*, oil on canvas, 1889

Seurat may well have used not only the chromatic circle but also the *rapporteur esthétique*, an instrument devised by Henry to decide whether or not a particular angle would prove harmonious: Dorra points out that this instrument was on sale commercially in 1889.

It was not quite possible, even so, for Seurat to subdue his own fancies. The combing of the horse's mane, for instance, releases those mysterious forms, part-cyclamen, part-butterfly, part-forked tongue and tail, which figure so largely in *Le Chahut*. These are echoed by the hands of the clown half-hidden by the ringmaster. The same cryptic winged forms recur in the collar and cap of the clown in the foreground (*Ills. 223, 224*), in the overcoat of the man in the fourth row from the top, and in the shoulder-knots of the rider. The very passivity of the cretinous mob is, once again, unmistakably a comment of Seurat's upon the herd which witnesses great feats of skill and discipline and takes them all for granted. (Here Apollinaire's remark should be remembered: that 'no painter so much reminds me of Molière, the Molière of *Le Bourgeois Gentilhomme*, as the Seurat of *Le Cirque*'.) And Claude Roger-Marx, whose father was almost the first to see merit in the *Baignade*, makes an exact historical point when he says that 'the young painters who pinned up, in 1910 or thereabouts, a photograph of the *Chahut* or the *Cirque* between two negro

222 *Le Chenal de Gravelines: Grand Fort-Philippe*, oil on canvas, 1890

masks were not enamoured of the use of pure colour or the *mélange optique*. They were grateful to Seurat for having equalled Cézanne in his rediscovery of the laws of style and composition, when he declared that the linear organization of a canvas was every bit as important as the organization of its colour.'

Le Cirque can be related to Cubism, and to art nouveau; and by the accident of Seurat's death it has lost its real character, that of a transitional and conceptual picture, and taken on a terminal appearance which was certainly not in Seurat's intentions. What he would have done later, no one can tell, but one thing is certain: that his was not the kind of gift that dies out or petrifies with age. Others might have fallen, and indeed did fall, into doctrinaire practice; by 1890 more than one member of the neo-impressionist group had seceded, and Henry van de Velde went so far as to speak of Seurat's 'shabby and distrustful' attitude to his associates. Pissarro had given up the dot as a bad job. Gauguin was in the ascendant. Within the next year or two it would have become clear that Seurat was either a one-idea man, or an artist who would have renewed himself throughout a career which might, given the life-span of Rouault or Matisse, have lasted until the liberation of France. As it was, he died at a particularly enigmatic moment in his evolution. On 20th March 1891, the Indépendants held their exhibition—one in which Seurat had taken an extremely active part; nine days later he died of an illness, as yet unidentified, which seems to have been a form of meningitis. Barely a fortnight later, his little son died of the same illness.

To one as discreet, and as orderly, as Seurat there would have been something peculiarly repulsive in the quarrels which broke out after his death, sundering friend from friend, setting a Kahn camp against a Signac camp, driving Madeleine Knobloch to turn everyone against her, and making it impossible to prepare, in good time and with the co-operation of all who knew him, a book which would have established once and for all the facts about his life, his character, and his career. Something was lost for ever in the lunatic days when the squabbles raged from Paris across to Brussels, where Seurat had many friends and admirers, and back again. But in the last twenty or thirty years devoted students have reconstituted much of that original information, and it is on their work that I have gratefully drawn.

Of Seurat's friends none had his gifts, or his power of sustained and systematic application, or his inwardness of mind. But the Signac of the 1880s, who had Seurat as his immediate mentor, is a very different thing from the Signac of later years. Cross got very near to the art of the future when he spoke to Théo van Rysselberghe of the 'idea of chromatic harmonies completely invented and

223 *Le Clown et Monsieur Loyal*, 1890. One of the few occasions on which Seurat is known to have used watercolour—the better, perhaps, to touch in a design which depended on the speed and exactitude of its linear disposition

Dernier dessin
de G. Seurat.

established, so to speak, without reference to nature as a point of departure'. Willy Finch, an Englishman by birth, and Théo van Rysselberghe, and Dubois-Pillet, all produced pictures of real distinction in the late 1880s. But when Seurat was no more than the lost leader, and when, after the death of his mother, the *Revue Blanche* organized an exhibition of Seurats for sale, it was difficult to get anyone but his old friends to buy them; and when, towards 1910 and later, his reputation began to climb towards its rightful level, it was the painters of a new generation who saw the point of his work: Delaunay, for instance, and Severini, and Juan Gris. Above all, however, Matisse saw through the superficial 'importance' of Seurat's career to the qualities which today endear him to us. And he did so not as an admirer or an imitator, but as one who had reacted against Seurat and carried the purposeful use of colour a stage further.

224 *Le Clown du Premier Plan*, 1890–1. Seurat later made a radical change in his treatment of the clown in the foreground. By making him turn his head sharply to the right, he made the whole of the lower half of the painting swing in one direction, while the upper half followed the headlong motion of the horse and its rider. The clown's head cap was made, moreover, to counterfeit the emblem of festivity which appears over and over again in *Le Chahut*

Writing in 1908, he said 'Divisionism was the first organised use of Impressionist method, but its organisation was purely physical and, often enough, merely mechanical. The division of colour led to the division of form and contour. A jerky surface resulted. As they turn greyer and greyer with age Seurat's paintings have lost the programmatic quality of their colour-arrangement: but they have kept their other, truer values—those human, painterly values which today seem ever more profound.'

Since 1908 a great deal has happened to our notions of colour, and we may agree with Matisse that Seurat's major late paintings 'turn greyer and greyer with age'. Certainly we should find it hard to accept what Signac said in 1899; that neo-impressionism 'guaranteed a maximum of luminosity, and of colour-harmony, which had never before been attained'. A case could be made out for those early panels in which every stroke of the brush has the wonder of convalescence; but on the whole we are almost relieved to put the whole question of colour on one side, for the paintings which, since Seurat, can best rival his in the majestic clarity of their architecture are the all but monochromatic masterpieces of analytical cubism by Picasso and Braque. But one of the remarkable things about Seurat's heritage is that there has turned out to be something in it for almost every subsequent artist of consequence. Analytical cubism took from *Le Cirque* the concept of space up-ended and brought close to the picture-plane; Art Nouveau, the eloquence of arabesque; Futurism, the notation of pure energy which Seurat perfected in *Le Chahut*; Orphism, the systematic use of pure divided colour. Marcel Duchamp, in his *Nude Descending a Staircase*, developed the idea of serial representation (already present in *Le Chahut*). Kandinsky wrote in *On the Spiritual in Art* that the theory of neo-impressionism was very near to abstract art. ('This theory, which the neo-impressionists regard as universal, does not consist in fixing upon canvas a fragment of Nature chosen at random, but in showing Nature complete and entire in all her splendour.') Robert Delaunay was careful to distinguish between the theories of colour with which Seurat concerned himself and the mechanism of the dot: the dot, he said, was 'merely a technical device, in no respect comparable in importance to the law of colour-contrast, which is a means to pure expression'. And Delaunay was as influential in Germany, before 1914, as he was in France: Klee, Macke and the young Max Ernst all learnt from him. An article by Klee, dated 1912, makes it plain that he had digested the colour-teaching of Seurat and Delaunay long before colour made a significant appearance in his own work; and later, in his Bauhaus courses, he urged upon his students the study of precisely the schemas from which Seurat's own practice was derived. Max Ernst put Seurat next to Piero della Francesca in his private Pantheon, long before scholarship had revealed the kinship between the two. Balthus produced in *Le Passage du Commerce* an urban landscape which can stand in Seurat's company and owes much to him both in the severity of its architecture and in the detached irony of its social observation. Seurat's practice leads logically to the idea, now so

225 Seurat's last painting, left unfinished at his death and bequeathed to the Louvre in 1926 by the great American collector John Quinn: *Le Cirque*, oil on canvas (73 by 59 inches)

widely current, of the painting as an autonomous object. At his hands it was the richer and more complex for being tied to identifiable subject-matter; but the notion of the paint-structure as the rival of nature was present in his work even when he was still following the classic Ecole des Beaux-Arts practice of going to Barbizon for his motifs.

Nor has his other lesson gone unheard: it is thanks to him, in the last analysis, that painters feel free to draw their material from whatever department of visual experience seems to them appropriate. Democracy in this domain is absolute, and the real artist can start from anywhere: this is not an idea which originated with Seurat, but it is one of the things that he has to teach us, and the trail which he started leads, directly or indirectly, to many of the major achievements of the last fifteen years. But for the coalescence of ideas both august and humble, for the 'human painterly values' which Matisse extolled, and for their organization in pictorial structures as grand as any in the history of art, Seurat has had no successor.

Short Bibliography

List of Illustrations

Index

Short Bibliography

Indispensable to any serious student of Seurat is César de Hauke's two-volume catalogue of the entire *œuvre*, published by Gründ, Paris, in 1962 and the source, as I have already acknowledged, of much that appears in this book. The Dorra-Rewald *Seurat* of 1959 (Les Beaux-Arts, Paris) catalogues the paintings only but includes a great deal of biographical and critical material.

Other publications in book-form include Gustave Coquiot's pioneering but erratic *Seurat* (1924), two studies by Lucie Cousturier (1922 and 1926), Gustave Kahn's *Les Dessins de Seurat* (1928), Rewald's earlier study of Seurat (New York, 1943, and Paris, 1948, in a revised edition), and Germain Seligman's *Drawings of Georges Seurat* (New York, 1945). Two powerful newcomers in the field are Robert L. Herbert's important study of the drawings of Seurat (Shorewood Publishers, Inc., New York, 1962, Studio Vista, London, 1965) and William Innes Homer's exhaustive *Seurat and the Science of Painting* (MIT Press, Cambridge, Mass., 1964). The Phaidon Press *Seurat* (1965) reprints an essay by Roger Fry on the subject and has an introduction by Sir Anthony Blunt.

References to important contributions by Fénéon, Signac, Robert Rey, Meyer Schapiro, Daniel C. Rich, André Chastel, Robert Goldwater, Robert L. Herbert, W. I. Homer, Benedict Nicolson, Aaron Scharf and others can be found in the extensive bibliographies which are a feature of several of the books listed above. Signac's *D'Eugène Delacroix au néo-impressionisme* was reprinted in a handy pocket edition by Miroirs de l'Art, Hermann, Paris in 1964, and an immense amount of relevant material has been marshalled by John Rewald in his *Post-Impressionism from Van Gogh to Gauguin* (New York, 2nd edition 1962).

List of Illustrations

Picture sizes are given in inches, height preceding width. The abbreviation CdH refers to César de Hauke's two-volume catalogue of Seurat's works

1 *Kneeling Figure* (after Poussin), 1875
Unsigned, dated l/l (CdH 224)
Black-lead, $20\frac{5}{8} \times 14\frac{13}{16}$
Private collection
Photo: courtesy César de Hauke

2 *Detail from the Parthenon Frieze*, 1875
Signed and dated l/r (CdH 220)
Black-lead, $18\frac{15}{16} \times 24\frac{7}{8}$
Private collection, Paris
Photo: courtesy César de Hauke

3 *Ulysse et les Prétendants*, 1876
Signed and dated l/r (CdH 233)
Black-lead, $9\frac{1}{16} \times 12\frac{5}{8}$
Formerly owned by Félix Fénéon
Photo: courtesy César de Hauke

4 *Séparation*, 1876
Signed and dated l/r (CdH 234)
Black-lead, $9\frac{11}{16} \times 12\frac{5}{8}$
Collection Mme Ginette Signac
Photo: courtesy César de Hauke

5 *Sainte Marthe, de profil*, *c.* 1876–8
Unsigned (CdH 259)
Black-lead, $23\frac{5}{8} \times 18\frac{3}{8}$
Private collection
Photo: courtesy César de Hauke

6 *Satyr and Goat*, *c.* 1877
Unsigned (CdH 299)
Charcoal, 25×19
Private collection
Photo: courtesy César de Hauke

7 *Homme Lisant sur un Terrasse*, *c.* 1884
Unsigned (CdH 599)
Conté crayon, $12\frac{1}{8} \times 9\frac{1}{4}$
Collection Mr and Mrs Robert B. Eichholz, Washington, D.C.
Photo: courtesy César de Hauke

8 *The Artist's Mother*, 1882–3
Unsigned (CdH 582)
Conté crayon, $12\frac{7}{8} \times 9\frac{1}{2}$
Metropolitan Museum of Art, New York
Photo: courtesy César de Hauke

9 *Mme Seurat, Lisant*, *c.* 1883
Unsigned (CdH 584)
Conté crayon (Dimensions unknown)
Formerly owned by Dikran Kelekian
Photo: courtesy César de Hauke

10 *Académie*, *c.* 1877
Unsigned (CdH 269)
Black-lead, $25\frac{1}{8} \times 18\frac{15}{16}$
Private collection
Photo: courtesy César de Hauke

11 *Mendiant Hindou*, *c.* 1878–9
Unsigned (CdH 282)
Black pencil, $18\frac{1}{8} \times 15\frac{3}{8}$
Private collection
Photo: courtesy César de Hauke

12 *Richard Southwell, after Holbein*, *c.* 1877
Unsigned (CdH 284)
Black-lead, $9\frac{11}{16} \times 7\frac{11}{16}$
Formerly owned by Paul Eluard
Photo: courtesy César de Hauke

13 *Jeune Fille*, *c.* 1876
Unsigned (CdH 236)
Black-lead, $11\frac{13}{16} \times 8\frac{1}{2}$
Private collection
Photo: courtesy César de Hauke

14 *Rade de Brest, Caserne, Divers Croquis*, *c.* 1880
Unsigned (CdH 360)
Black-lead and coloured pencils, $5\frac{7}{8} \times 8\frac{15}{16}$
Collection André Lhote
Photo: courtesy César de Hauke

15 *Quatre Personnages, Un Assis*, *c.* 1880
(CdH 344)
Black-lead, $5\frac{15}{16} \times 9\frac{1}{2}$
Formerly owned by Paul Valéry
Photo: courtesy César de Hauke

16 *Un Bonhomme*, *c.* 1881
Unsigned (CdH 411)
Paint-brush, $4\frac{3}{4} \times 1\frac{9}{16}$
Collection Mme Camille Platteel
Photo: courtesy César de Hauke

17 *Cireur de Bottes, c.* 1880–1
Unsigned (CdH 409)
Black-lead, 3 $\frac{13}{16}$ × 4 $\frac{5}{16}$
Collection Mme Ginette Signac
Photo: courtesy César de Hauke

18 *Boy Standing near a Lamp, c.* 1884
Unsigned (CdH 449)
Conté crayon, 11 × 8 $\frac{3}{4}$
Collection Robert Lebel
Photo: courtesy César de Hauke

19 *Allusion au Pauvre Pêcheur, c.* 1881
Unsigned (CdH 6)
Oil on board, 6 $\frac{1}{2}$ × 10 $\frac{1}{16}$
Collection Mme Huguette Bérès
Photo: courtesy César de Hauke

20 *Femme Accoudée à un Parapet de la Seine,*
c. 1881
Unsigned (CdH 462)
Conté crayon, 9 $\frac{3}{8}$ × 6 $\frac{1}{4}$
Collection Pierre Angrand
Photo: courtesy César de Hauke

21 *Tambourineur à Montfermeil, c.* 1881
Unsigned (CdH 442)
Conté crayon, 9 × 7
Private collection
Photo: courtesy César de Hauke

22 *Aman Jean, c.* 1883
Unsigned (CdH 588)
Conté crayon, 24 $\frac{3}{4}$ × 18 $\frac{3}{4}$
Metropolitan Museum of Art, New York
Photo: courtesy César de Hauke

23 *Doux Pays*, by Pierre Puvis de
Chavannes
Oil on canvas, 10 $\frac{1}{4}$ × 18 $\frac{5}{8}$
Yale University Art Gallery, Abbey Fund
Photo: courtesy Yale University Art
Gallery

24 *Cheval Noir et Personnages, c.* 1883
Unsigned (CdH 85)
Oil on board, 5 $\frac{13}{16}$ × 9 $\frac{11}{16}$
Formerly owned by Mme Vve Léopold
Appert
Photo: courtesy César de Hauke

25 *Le Labourage, c.* 1883
Unsigned (CdH 525)
Conté crayon, 10 $\frac{5}{8}$ × 12 $\frac{5}{8}$
Louvre, Paris
Photo: courtesy César de Hauke

26 *Les Deux Charrettes, c.* 1883
Unsigned (CdH 532)
Conté crayon, 9 $\frac{1}{2}$ × 12 $\frac{5}{16}$
Collection Mme Alph. Bellier
Photo: courtesy César de Hauke

27 *Cavalier sur une Route, c.* 1883
Unsigned (CdH 518)
Conté crayon, 9 $\frac{1}{2}$ × 12 $\frac{5}{16}$
Formerly owned by Dr Albert
Charpentier
Photo: courtesy César de Hauke

28 *Le Cheval au Tombereau, c.* 1883
Unsigned (CdH 531)
Conté crayon on white paper, 9 $\frac{1}{2}$ × 12 $\frac{5}{16}$
Louvre, Paris
Photo: courtesy César de Hauke

29 *Paysans aux Champs, c.* 1883
Unsigned (CdH 528)
Conté crayon, 9 $\frac{5}{16}$ × 11 $\frac{5}{8}$
Collection Mme Bela Hein
Photo: courtesy César de Hauke

30 *Au Travail de la Terre, c.* 1883
Unsigned (CdH 562)
Conté crayon, 9 $\frac{3}{4}$ × 12 $\frac{1}{4}$
Louvre, Paris
Photo: courtesy César de Hauke

31 *L'Homme à la Pioche, c.* 1883
Unsigned (CdH 552)
Conté crayon, 9 $\frac{1}{2}$ × 12 $\frac{5}{16}$
Formerly owned by Félix Fénéon
Photo: courtesy César de Hauke

32 *Les Glaneuses*, 1857, by Jean-François
Millet
Oil on canvas, 33 × 44
Louvre, Paris
Photo: Collection Viollet

33 *Paysannes au travail, c.* 1883
Unsigned (CdH 60)
Oil on canvas, 15 $\frac{1}{8}$ × 18 $\frac{1}{4}$
The Solomon R. Guggenheim Museum
Collection
Photo: courtesy Guggenheim Museum

34 *La Meule de Foin, c.* 1883
Unsigned (CdH 44)
Oil on canvas, 14 $\frac{3}{4}$ × 17 $\frac{3}{4}$
Private collection
Photo: Routhier

35 *Maisons et Jardin, c.* 1882
Unsigned (CdH 19)
Oil on canvas, 10 $\frac{7}{8}$ × 18 $\frac{1}{4}$
Private collection
Photo: Routhier

36 *Dans un Pré*, *c.* 1883
Unsigned (CdH 48)
Oil on board, $6\frac{1}{2} \times 9\frac{7}{8}$
Yale University Art Gallery
Photo: courtesy César de Hauke

37 *Du Linge sur un Cordeau*, *c.* 1883
Unsigned (CdH 541)
Conté crayon, $11\frac{13}{16} \times 8\frac{11}{16}$
Collection Pierre Lévy, France
Photo: courtesy Art Institute of Chicago

38 *Paysanne les Mains au Sol*, *c.* 1882
Unsigned (CdH 474)
Conté crayon, $9\frac{3}{8} \times 6\frac{1}{2}$
Collection Mr and Mrs Paul Mellon, Upperville, Virginia
Photo: courtesy César de Hauke

39 *Casseur de Pierres*, *c.* 1883
Unsigned (CdH 555)
Conté crayon, $12\frac{3}{16} \times 9\frac{1}{2}$
Formerly owned by Maurice Appert
Photo: courtesy César de Hauke

40 *Ville d'Avray, Maisons Blanches*, *c.* 1882
Unsigned (CdH 20)
Oil on canvas, $13 \times 18\frac{1}{8}$
Photo: courtesy Walker Art Gallery, Liverpool

41 *Figure Massive dans un Paysage à Barbizon*, *c.* 1882
Unsigned (CdH 25)
Oil on board, $6\frac{1}{8} \times 9\frac{7}{8}$
Collection Dr Rignault
Photo: courtesy César de Hauke

42 *Vaches dans un Pré*, *c.* 1883
Unsigned (CdH 49)
Oil on board, $6\frac{1}{8} \times 9\frac{1}{2}$
Private collection
Photo: courtesy César de Hauke

43 *Le Chemin Creux*, *c.* 1882
Unsigned (CdH 29)
Oil on canvas, $12\frac{7}{8} \times 15\frac{1}{2}$
Private collection
Photo: John Webb

44 *Paysan au Travail*, *c.* 1883
Unsigned (CdH 61)
Oil on board, $6\frac{11}{16} \times 9\frac{7}{8}$
Private collection, Paris
Photo: Jacqueline Hyde

45 *Le Jardinier*, *c.* 1882
Unsigned (CdH 37)
Oil on canvas, $14\frac{9}{16} \times 17\frac{3}{4}$
Photo: courtesy César de Hauke

46 *Vers le Bourg*, *c.* 1883
Unsigned (CdH 54)
Oil on board, $6\frac{3}{8} \times 9\frac{7}{8}$
Private collection, Paris
Photo: Routhier

47 *La Charrette Attelée*, *c.* 1883
Unsigned (CdH 46)
Oil on canvas, $13 \times 16\frac{1}{8}$
The Solomon R. Guggenheim Museum Collection
Photo: courtesy Guggenheim Museum

48 *Les Terrassiers*, *c.* 1883
Unsigned (CdH 62)
Oil on board, $5\frac{7}{8} \times 9\frac{1}{2}$
Collection Mr and Mrs Paul Mellon, Upperville, Virginia
Photo: David Robb

49 *Fort de la Halle*, *c.* 1882
Unsigned (CdH 484)
Conté crayon, $12\frac{3}{8} \times 9\frac{7}{8}$
Private collection
Photo: courtesy César de Hauke

50 *Les Deux Campagnards*, *c.* 1883
Unsigned (CdH 523)
Conté crayon, $8\frac{1}{4} \times 10\frac{7}{8}$
Collection Miss Adelaide M. de Groot, New York
Photo: courtesy César de Hauke

51 *Le Poulain*, *c.* 1883
Unsigned (CdH 527)
Conté crayon, 9×12
Collection Robert Lehman, New York
Photo: courtesy César de Hauke

52 *Attelage près d'Arbres Grêles*, *c.* 1883
Unsigned (CdH 530)
Conté crayon, $8\frac{7}{8} \times 11\frac{13}{16}$
Formerly owned by Henri le Savoureux
Photo: courtesy César de Hauke

53 *Le Carriole et le Chien*, *c.* 1883
Unsigned (CdH 543)
Conté crayon, 12×9
Collection Princess Marguerite Caetani, Rome
Photo: courtesy César de Hauke

54 *Dans la Rue*, *c.* 1883
Unsigned (CdH 516)
Conté crayon, $12\frac{5}{8} \times 9\frac{1}{16}$
Collection Mme Georges Bodenheimer
Photo: courtesy César de Hauke

55 *Les Vaches, c.* 1881
Unsigned (CdH 448)
Conté crayon, $9\frac{1}{16} \times 11\frac{1}{4}$
Formerly owned by Pierre Bonnard
Photo: courtesy César de Hauke

56 *Le Glaneur, c.* 1883
Unsigned (CdH 559)
Conté crayon, $12\frac{5}{8} \times 9\frac{1}{2}$
British Museum, London
Photo: courtesy César de Hauke

57 *Usines sous la Lune, c.* 1883
Unsigned (CdH 536)
Conté crayon, $8\frac{11}{16} \times 11\frac{1}{16}$
Collection Grégoire Tarnopol, New York
Photo: courtesy César de Hauke

58 *Lecture, c.* 1883–4
Signed u/l (CdH 585)
Conté crayon, $12\frac{1}{8} \times 9\frac{1}{2}$
Private collection
Photo: courtesy César de Hauke

59 *Soldat, vu de dos, Croquis de Mains et de Personnages, c.* 1880
Unsigned (CdH 368)
Black-lead and coloured pencils, $5\frac{11}{16} \times 9\frac{1}{2}$
Collection Benedict Nicolson, London
Photo: John Webb

60 *Dans la Rue, c.* 1883
Unsigned (CdH 69)
Oil on board, $6\frac{1}{2} \times 9\frac{3}{4}$
Private collection
Photo: courtesy César de Hauke

61 *Frileuse, Tête de Profil, c.* 1877
Unsigned (CdH 306)
Black-lead (Dimensions unknown)
Formerly owned by Félix Fénéon
Photo: courtesy César de Hauke

62 *Le Berger Endormie, c.* 1878
Unsigned (CdH 310)
Black-lead, $9\frac{1}{2} \times 13$
Louvre, Paris
Photo: courtesy César de Hauke

63 *La Jambe,* 1883–4
Unsigned (CdH 594)
Conté crayon, $9\frac{1}{16} \times 11\frac{11}{16}$
Collection Gerard Bonnier, Stockholm
Photo: courtesy César de Hauke

64 *Soldat Assis dans l'Herbe, un Debout, un Bateau, c.* 1880
Unsigned (CdH 370)
Black-lead and coloured pencils, $5\frac{11}{16} \times 9\frac{1}{2}$
Formerly owned by Félix Fénéon
Photo: courtesy César de Hauke

65 *Un Cordonnier, c.* 1879–80
Unsigned (CdH 332)
Black-lead, $4\frac{1}{16} \times 4\frac{11}{16}$
Collection Mr and Mrs Robert L. Herbert
Photo: courtesy César de Hauke

66 *Le Clown Rouge, c.* 1880
Unsigned (CdH 385)
Coloured pencil, $5\frac{3}{4} \times 9\frac{1}{16}$
Formerly owned by Mme Camille Platteel
Photo: courtesy César de Hauke

67 *Banquistes, c.* 1880
Unsigned (CdH 384)
Coloured pencil, $5\frac{3}{4} \times 9\frac{1}{16}$
Photo: courtesy César de Hauke

68 *Danseuse de Corvi, c.* 1880
Unsigned (CdH 381)
Conté crayon, $7\frac{11}{16} \times 4\frac{1}{16}$
Formerly owned by Mme Camille Platteel
Photo: courtesy César de Hauke

69 *Convulsionnaires de Tanger (five sketches with notes),* 1881
Unsigned (CdH 386)
Pen-and-ink, $8\frac{11}{16} \times 12\frac{1}{16}$
Collection Mme Ginette Signac
Photo: courtesy César de Hauke

70 *A Demi Couchée, c.* 1881
Signed l/l (CdH 436)
Black pencil, $7\frac{1}{8} \times 9\frac{1}{16}$
Formerly owned by Jacques Rodrigues-Henriqués
Photo: courtesy César de Hauke

71 *Assise les Mains Croisées, c.* 1881
Unsigned (CdH 429)
Conté crayon, $6\frac{3}{4} \times 4\frac{1}{2}$
Collection Giorgio Morandi, Bologna
Photo: courtesy César de Hauke

72 *Réparant son Manteau, c.* 1880–1
Unsigned (CdH 403)
Black-lead, $6\frac{1}{2} \times 4\frac{1}{8}$
Collection Mr and Mrs R. J. Sainsbury, London
Photo: courtesy César de Hauke

73 *Coseuseu, un Tableau au Mur, c.* 1881
Unsigned (CdH 446)
Conté crayon, $9\frac{1}{16} \times 7\frac{1}{2}$
Formerly owned by Percy M. Turner, London
Photo: courtesy César de Hauke

74 *Cireur de Bottes et son Client, c.* 1881
Unsigned (CdH 447)
Conté crayon, $5\frac{1}{2} \times 4\frac{5}{16}$
Private collection
Photo: courtesy César de Hauke

75 *Groupe de Gens, c.* 1883
Unsigned (CdH 550)
Conté crayon on white paper, $9\frac{1}{2} \times 12\frac{3}{16}$
Louvre, Paris
Photo: courtesy César de Hauke

76 *Suivant le Sentier, c.* 1883
Unsigned (CdH 548)
Conté crayon, $12\frac{3}{16} \times 9\frac{1}{16}$
Formerly owned by Maurice Appert
Photo: courtesy César de Hauke

77 *Maisons (Effet de Soleil—Paysage aux Maisons), c.* 1881
Unsigned (CdH 455)
Conté crayon, $9\frac{1}{4} \times 12\frac{1}{8}$
Collection Mr and Mrs Walter C. Baker, New York
Photo: courtesy César de Hauke

78 *Casseur de Pierres et Autres Personnages—Le Raincy, c.* 1881
Unsigned (CdH 463)
Conté crayon, $12\frac{1}{8} \times 14\frac{3}{4}$
Collection Museum of Modern Art, New York
Photo: Museum of Modern Art

79 *Crépuscule du Soir, c.* 1883
Unsigned (CdH 522)
Conté crayon, $9\frac{1}{16} \times 11\frac{13}{16}$
Galerie Berggruen, Paris
Photo: courtesy César de Hauke

80 *La Route de la Gare, c.* 1882
Unsigned (CdH 472)
Conté crayon, $9\frac{1}{2} \times 11\frac{13}{16}$
Collection Ivo Hauptmann, Altona
Photo: courtesy César de Hauke

81 *La Voie Ferrée, c.* 1882
Unsigned (CdH 471)
Conté crayon, $9\frac{1}{16} \times 12$
Formerly owned by Henri le Savoureux
Photo: courtesy César de Hauke

82 *Locomotive, c.* 1882
Unsigned (CdH 478)
Conté crayon, $9\frac{7}{8} \times 12\frac{5}{8}$
Collection Charles Gillet
Photo: courtesy César de Hauke

83 *Place de la Concorde, l'Hiver, c.* 1883
Unsigned (CdH 564)
Conté crayon touched up with chalk, $9\frac{1}{8} \times 12\frac{1}{8}$
The Solomon R. Guggenheim Museum Collection
Photo: courtesy César de Hauke

84 *Place de la Concorde, c.* 1883
Unsigned (CdH 563)
Conté crayon, $9\frac{11}{16} \times 12\frac{3}{8}$
Private collection
Photo: courtesy César de Hauke

85 *La Zone, c.* 1883
Unsigned (CdH 521)
Conté crayon, $8\frac{5}{8} \times 11\frac{5}{8}$
Collection Alex Loeb
Photo: courtesy César de Hauke

86 *Le Chiffonier, c.* 1883
Unsigned (CdH 520)
Conté crayon, $9\frac{1}{2} \times 12\frac{3}{16}$
Formerly owned by Mme Berthe Paul Signac
Photo: courtesy César de Hauke

87 *L'Échafaudage, c.* 1883
Unsigned (CdH 567)
Conté crayon, $12\frac{1}{2} \times 9\frac{1}{8}$
Collection Mme Ginette Signac
Photo: courtesy César de Hauke

88 *Le Fiacre, c.* 1885
Unsigned (CdH 647)
Conté crayon, $9\frac{1}{4} \times 12$
Collection Sydney J. Lamon, New York
Photo: courtesy César de Hauke

89 *Le Couvreur, c.* 1883
Unsigned (CdH 565)
Conté crayon, $12\frac{3}{16} \times 9\frac{1}{2}$
Louvre, Paris
Photo: courtesy César de Hauke

90 *Rencontre, c.* 1882
Signed l/l (CdH 477)
Conté crayon, $9\frac{1}{16} \times 12\frac{3}{16}$
Private collection
Photo: courtesy César de Hauke

91 *Soir Familial, c.* 1883
Unsigned (CdH 576)
Conté crayon, $9\frac{1}{2} \times 12\frac{13}{16}$
Dudley Peter Allen Memorial Art Museum, Oberlin College
Photo: courtesy César de Hauke

92 *Devant le Balcon, c.* 1883–4
Unsigned (CdH 587)
Conté crayon, $12\frac{3}{16} \times 9\frac{1}{2}$
Louvre, Paris
Photo: courtesy César de Hauke

93 *Le Dineur, c.* 1884
Signed l/r (CdH 600)
Conté crayon touched up with gauoche,
$12\frac{1}{2} \times 8\frac{5}{8}$
Private collection
Photo: courtesy César de Hauke

94 *Le Chat, c.* 1883
Unsigned (CdH 574)
Conté crayon, $9\frac{1}{16} \times 12$
Galerie Berggruen, Paris
Photo: courtesy César de Hauke

95 *Par la Grille du Balcon, c.* 1883–4
Unsigned (CdH 586)
Conté crayon, $12\frac{3}{16} \times 9\frac{1}{2}$
Collection Mme W. Feilchenfeldt,
Zurich

96 *Troncs d'Arbres Reflétés dans l'Eau, c.* 1883
Unsigned (CdH 553)
Conté crayon, $9\frac{1}{2} \times 12\frac{5}{8}$
Collection Mme Jaeggli-Hahnloser,
Winterthur
Photo: courtesy César de Hauke

97 *Deux Hommes Marchant dans un Champ,
c.* 1883
Unsigned (CdH 524)
Black pencil, $12 \times 9\frac{1}{4}$
Baltimore Museum of Art
Photo: courtesy César de Hauke

98 *Le Cocher de Fiacre, c.* 1882
(CdH 481)
Conté crayon, $9\frac{11}{16} \times 12\frac{3}{16}$
Collection Mme Huguette Bérès
Photo: courtesy Mme Bérès

99 *L'Homme à la Houe, c.* 1883
Unsigned (CdH 558)
Conté crayon, $12\frac{5}{8} \times 9\frac{1}{2}$
Louvre, Paris
Photo: courtesy César de Hauke

100 *Maison sous les Arbres, c.* 1883
Unsigned (CdH 547)
Conté crayon, $11\frac{13}{16} \times 8\frac{11}{16}$
Buchholz Gallery, New York
Photo: courtesy César de Hauke

101 *Sous-Bois à Pontaubert, c.* 1883–7
Unsigned (CdH 14)
Oil on canvas, $30\frac{3}{4} \times 24\frac{13}{16}$
Private collection
Photo: John Webb

102 *Banlieue sous la Neige, c.* 1883
Unsigned (CdH 72)
Oil on board, $6\frac{1}{8} \times 9\frac{1}{2}$
Collection Comtesse de Ganay, Paris
Photo: Routhier

103 *Ruines des Tuileries, c.* 1882
Unsigned (CdH 13)
Oil on board, $6\frac{3}{8} \times 9\frac{7}{8}$
Formerly owned by J. Hessel
Photo: courtesy César de Hauke

104 *Maisons dans les Arbres, c.* 1883
Unsigned (CdH 56)
Oil on board, $6\frac{3}{8} \times 9\frac{7}{8}$
Reproduced by courtesy of the Glasgow
Art Gallery and Museum

105 *Casseur de Pierres à la Brouette—Le
Raincy, c.* 1883
Unsigned, red cachet l/r (CdH 100)
Oil on board, $6\frac{3}{8} \times 10$
The Phillips Collection
Photo: Phillips Collection

106 *Le Faucheur, c.* 1883
Unsigned (CdH 58)
Oil on board, $6\frac{1}{2} \times 9\frac{7}{8}$
Collection Robert Lehman, New York
Photo: courtesy Robert Lehman

107 *Paysan à la Houe, c.* 1883
Unsigned (CdH 103)
Oil on canvas, $18\frac{1}{8} \times 22$
The Solomon R. Guggenheim Museum
Collection
Photo: courtesy Guggenheim Museum

108 *La Vespasienne, c.* 1882
Unsigned (CdH 40)
Oil on board, $9\frac{1}{4} \times 6$
Collection Daniel Wildenstein, New
York
Photo: courtesy César de Hauke

109 *Banlieue, c.* 1883
Unsigned (CdH 75)
Oil on canvas, $12\frac{3}{4} \times 16\frac{1}{4}$
Collection Pierre Lévy, France

110 *Paysanne Assise dans l'Herbe, c.* 1883
Unsigned (CdH 59)
Oil on canvas, $15 \times 18\frac{1}{4}$
The Solomon R. Guggenheim Museum
Collection
Photo: courtesy Guggenheim Museum

111 *Petit Paysan Assis dans un Pré, c.* 1882
Unsigned (CdH 15)
Oil on canvas, $25\frac{5}{8} \times 31\frac{7}{8}$
Reproduced by courtesy of the Glasgow
Art Gallery and Museum

112 *Nu Assis*, *c.* 1883–4
(CdH 598)
Conté crayon, $12\frac{3}{8} \times 9\frac{1}{2}$
Collection S. A. Morrison, London
Photo: courtesy César de Hauke

113 *Homme Peignant son Bateau*, *c.* 1883
Unsigned (CdH 66)
Oil on board, $6\frac{3}{8} \times 9\frac{1}{2}$
Collection Lord Butler
Photo: John Webb

114 *Les Deux Rives*, *c.* 1883
Unsigned (CdH 79)
Oil on board, $6\frac{3}{8} \times 9\frac{7}{8}$
Reproduced by courtesy of the Glasgow Art Gallery and Museum

115 *Cinq Figures d'Hommes*, *c.* 1883
(CdH 82)
Oil on board, $5\frac{15}{16} \times 9\frac{7}{8}$
Formerly owned by Maurice Denis
Photo: courtesy César de Hauke

116 *La Seine*, *c.* 1883
Unsigned (CdH 83)
Oil on board, $6\frac{3}{8} \times 9\frac{7}{8}$
Private collection, Paris
Photo: Routhier

117 *Cheval Blanc dans l'Eau*, *c.* 1883
Unsigned (CdH 87)
Oil on board, $6\frac{3}{8} \times 9\frac{7}{8}$
Private collection, Paris
Photo: Jacqueline Hyde

118 *Personnages Assis et Étendus, Cheval Noir*, *c.* 1883
Unsigned, cachet l/l (CdH 88)
Oil on board, $6\frac{3}{8} \times 9\frac{7}{8}$
National Gallery of Scotland, Edinburgh
Photo: Tom Scott

119 *Homme Portant un Chapeau de Paille, Assis sur l'Herbe*, 1883–4
Signed u/r (CdH 595)
Conté crayon, $9\frac{1}{2} \times 11\frac{13}{16}$
Yale University Art Gallery
Photo: courtesy César de Hauke

120 *Homme Couché*, 1883–4
Unsigned (CdH 592)
Conté crayon, $9\frac{1}{8} \times 12\frac{5}{8}$
Collection Dr J. Koerfer, Bollingen, Berne
Photo: courtesy César de Hauke

121 *Cheval Blanc et Cheval Noir dans l'Eau*, *c.* 1883–4
Unsigned (CdH 86)
Oil on board, $6\frac{3}{8} \times 9\frac{7}{8}$
Collection Christabel Lady Aberconway, London
Photo: John Webb

122 *La Seine et Baigneur Nu assis sur la Berge*, *c.* 1883
Unsigned (CdH 91)
Oil on board, $6\frac{1}{4} \times 9\frac{3}{4}$
William Rockhill Nelson Gallery of Art, Kansas City
Photo: courtesy Kansas City Gallery of Art

123 *L'Homme Assis*, *c.* 1883
Unsigned (CdH 80)
Oil on board, $6\frac{11}{16} \times 10\frac{7}{16}$
Cleveland Museum of Art (Leonard C. Hanna, Jr., Collection)
Photo: Cleveland Museum

124 *Baignade*, *c.* 1883
(CdH 93)
Name of painter l/l
Oil on board, $6\frac{1}{4} \times 9\frac{3}{4}$
Collection Dr and Mrs David M. Levy, New York
Photo: Lerner

125 *Le Dormeur, Torse*, 1883–4
Unsigned (CdH 590)
Conté crayon, $9\frac{3}{8} \times 12\frac{1}{4}$
Louvre, Paris
Photo: courtesy César de Hauke

126 *L'Homme Couché*, 1883–4
Unsigned (CdH 589)
Conté crayon, $9\frac{1}{2} \times 12\frac{3}{16}$
Collection M. E. Beyeler, Basle
Photo: courtesy César de Hauke

127 *Une Baignade à Asnières*, 1883–4
Signed l/l (CdH 92)
Oil on canvas, $79 \times 118\frac{1}{2}$
National Gallery, London

128 *Paysage aux Arbres*, 1884–5
Unsigned (CdH 620)
Black-lead, $18\frac{1}{2} \times 24$
Private collection
Photo: courtesy César de Hauke

129 *Arbres sur les Berges de la Seine*, 1884–5
Unsigned (CdH 619)
Conté crayon, $24\frac{1}{4} \times 18\frac{3}{8}$
Private collection
Photo: courtesy César de Hauke

130 *Nourrice Debout, un Enfant dans les Bras, c.* 1882
Unsigned (CdH 488)
Conté crayon, $11\frac{13}{16} \times 9\frac{1}{16}$
Collection Albert Rothbart
Photo: courtesy César de Hauke

131 Sketch for *Le Grande Jatte*, 1884–5
Signed l/l, dated 1884 (CdH 131)
Oil on canvas, $25\frac{1}{2} \times 32$
Collection Mr and Mrs John Hay Whitney
Photo: courtesy Paul Rosenberg

132 *Paysage*, 1884–5
Signed l/r (CdH 641)
Conté crayon, $15\frac{3}{4} \times 23\frac{3}{4}$
Private collection
Photo: courtesy César de Hauke

133 *Un Dimanche d'Été à l'Ile de la Grande Jatte*, 1886
Signed l/r (CdH 162)
Oil on canvas, $81 \times 120\frac{3}{8}$
The Art Institute of Chicago, Helen Birch Bartlett Memorial Collection

134 *La Nounou*, 1884–5
Unsigned (CdH 630)
Conté crayon, 9×12
Collection M. A. Conger Goodyear, Westbury, Connecticut
Photo: courtesy César de Hauke

135 *Paysage et Personnages*, 1884–5
Unsigned (CdH 121)
Oil on board, $6\frac{1}{4} \times 10\frac{1}{4}$
Private collection, Paris
Photo: Jacqueline Hyde

136 *Promeneuse, c.* 1882
Unsigned (CdH 500)
Conté crayon, $12\frac{3}{16} \times 9\frac{7}{8}$
Formerly owned by Simon Benatov
Photo: courtesy César de Hauke

137 *La Promeneuse au Réverbère, c.* 1882
Unsigned (CdH 510)
Conté crayon, $12\frac{3}{16} \times 9\frac{1}{16}$
Collection M. S. van Deventer
Photo: courtesy César de Hauke

138 *Femmes au Bord de l'Eau*, 1884–5
Signed l/l (CdH 116)
Oil on board, $6\frac{1}{4} \times 9\frac{7}{8}$
Mr and Mrs Richard J. Bernhard, New York
Photo: Taylor and Dull

139 *Le Nœud Noir, c.* 1882
Unsigned (CdH 511)
Conté crayon, $12\frac{3}{16} \times 9\frac{1}{16}$
Private collection
Photo: courtesy César de Hauke

140 *Femme Debout, la Tête Nue, c.* 1882
Unsigned (CdH 505)
Conté crayon, $11\frac{13}{16} \times 8\frac{3}{8}$
Collection Mme Vve Olivier Sainsère
Photo: courtesy César de Hauke

141 *Artiste, c.* 1882
Unsigned (CdH 497)
Conté crayon, $12\frac{3}{16} \times 9\frac{1}{2}$
Formerly owned by Henri Matisse
Photo: courtesy César de Hauke

142 *Nourrice, c.* 1882
Unsigned (CdH 486)
Conté crayon, $12\frac{5}{8} \times 9\frac{7}{8}$
Collection Paul Rosenberg, New York
Photo: courtesy César de Hauke

143 *Groupes de Personnages*, 1884–5
Unsigned (CdH 117)
Oil on board, $6\frac{1}{8} \times 9\frac{3}{8}$
The collection of Robert Lehman, New York
Photo: courtesy Robert Lehman

144 *Figures Assises*, 1884–5
Unsigned, cachet l/r (CdH 123)
Oil on board, $6\frac{3}{8} \times 9\frac{11}{16}$
Courtesy the Fogg Art Museum, Harvard University

145 *La Jeune Fille dans l'Atelier, c.* 1887
Unsigned (CdH 601)
Conté crayon, $12\frac{1}{8} \times 9\frac{1}{2}$
Courtesy the Fogg Art Museum, Harvard University
Photo: courtesy César de Hauke

146 *La Pêcheuse à la Ligne*, 1884–5
Unsigned (CdH 635)
Conté crayon, $12\frac{1}{8} \times 9\frac{3}{8}$
Metropolitan Museum of Art. Purchased 1951 from the Museum of Modern Art, Lizzie P. Bliss Collection

147 *Les Jeunes Filles*, 1884–5
Unsigned (CdH 633)
Conté crayon, $9\frac{1}{4} \times 12$
Smith College Museum of Art
Photo: courtesy César de Hauke

148 *Sept Singes*, 1884–5
Unsigned (CdH 639)
Conté crayon, $11\frac{7}{8} \times 9\frac{1}{4}$
Louvre, Paris
Photo: courtesy César de Hauke

149 *Allegory*, by Lorenzo Costa
Signed l/r
Oil on canvas
Louvre, Paris
Photo: Agraci

150 *Le Couple*, 1884–5
Unsigned (CdH 136)
Oil on board, $9\frac{3}{4} \times 6\frac{3}{8}$
Private collection
Photo: courtesy César de Hauke

151 *Esquisse d'Ensemble*, 1884–5
Unsigned (CdH 142)
Oil on canvas, $26\frac{3}{4} \times 41$
Metropolitan Museum of Art, New York. Bequest of Samuel A. Lewisohn

152 *Fillette au Chapeau Niniche*, *c.* 1883
Unsigned (CdH 573)
Conté crayon, $12\frac{1}{2} \times 9\frac{1}{2}$
Collection Mr and Mrs Germain Seligman, New York
Photo: courtesy César de Hauke

153 *L'Enfant Blanc*, 1884–5
Unsigned (CdH 631)
Conté crayon, $12 \times 9\frac{1}{4}$
The Solomon R. Guggenheim Museum Collection
Photo: courtesy César de Hauke

154 *Petite Esquisse*, 1884–5
Unsigned (CdH 128)
Oil on board, $6 \times 9\frac{3}{4}$
Collection Mr and Mrs Leigh B. Block, Chicago

155 *Arbre et Homme*, *c.* 1884
Unsigned (CdH 616)
Conté crayon, $24 \times 18\frac{1}{8}$
Stadtische Museum, Wuppertal
Photo: courtesy César de Hauke

156 *Petite Esquisse*, 1884–5
Unsigned (CdH 120)
Oil on board, $6 \times 9\frac{1}{2}$
Collection Mr and Mrs Howard J. Sachs, New York

157 *Le Couple*, *c.* 1884–5
Unsigned (CdH 644)
Conté crayon, $11\frac{1}{2} \times 9$
Private collection, Paris
Photo: courtesy César de Hauke

158 *Deux Voiliers à Grandcamp*, *c.* 1885
Unsigned (CdH 150)
Oil on board, $6\frac{3}{8} \times 9\frac{7}{8}$
Copyright 1965 the Barnes Foundation

159 *Le Bec du Hoc à Grandcamp*, 1885
Signed l/r (CdH 159)
Oil on canvas, $26 \times 32\frac{1}{2}$
The Tate Gallery, London

160 *Grandcamp, Un Soir*, 1885
Signed l/l
Oil on canvas, $25\frac{5}{8} \times 32$
Collection Mr and Mrs John Hay Whitney

161 *Le Fort Samson à Grandcamp*, 1885
Unsigned (CdH 156)
Oil on board, $6\frac{1}{8} \times 9\frac{1}{2}$
Collection Mme Ginette Signac
Photo: courtesy César de Hauke

162 *Couché sous un Pont*, *c.* 1885
Unsigned (CdH 645)
Conté crayon, $9\frac{1}{2} \times 12\frac{3}{16}$
Collection Mme Ginette Signac, Paris
Photo: courtesy César de Hauke

163 *La Rade de Grandcamp*, 1885
Signed l/r (CdH 160)
Oil on canvas, $25\frac{5}{8} \times 32$
Private collection

164 Detail from *Un Dimanche d'Été à l'Ile de la Grande Jatte*
(See *Ill.* 133)

165 *Bout de la jetée à Honfleur*, 1886
Signed l/r (CdH 170)
Oil on canvas, $18\frac{1}{8} \times 21\frac{1}{4}$
Courtesy Rijksmuseum Kröller-Müller

166 *Entrée du port de Honfleur*, 1886
Signed l/l (CdH 171)
Oil on canvas, $21\frac{1}{4} \times 25\frac{5}{8}$
Copyright 1965 the Barnes Foundation

167 *La 'Maria' à Honfleur*, 1886
Signed l/l (CdH 164)
Oil on canvas, $21\frac{7}{16} \times 25\frac{3}{8}$
Museum of Modern Art, Prague

168 *Coin d'un Bassin (Honfleur)*, 1886
Signed l/l (CdH 163)
Oil on canvas, $31\frac{7}{8} \times 25\frac{5}{8}$
Rijksmuseum Kröller-Müller

169 *Le Peintre au Travail*, *c.* 1884
Unsigned (CdH 602)
Conté crayon, $12\frac{1}{8} \times 9$
Philadelphia Museum of Art
Photo: courtesy César de Hauke

170 *Écluse dans Paris*, *c.* 1884
Unsigned (CdH 608)
Conté crayon, $9 \times 11\frac{1}{4}$
Collection Mr and Mrs Sidney Simon, New York
Photo: courtesy César de Hauke

171 *Embouchure de la Seine un Soir, Honfleur*, 1886
Signed l/r (CdH 167)
Oil on canvas, $25\frac{1}{4} \times 31\frac{1}{2}$
Collection Museum of Modern Art, New York

172 *La Grève du Bas Butin à Honfleur*, 1886
Unsigned (CdH 169)
Oil on canvas, $26\frac{3}{8} \times 30\frac{3}{4}$
Musée des Beaux-Arts, Tournai
Photo: Jules Messiaen, Tournai

173 *La Tour Eiffel*, 1889
Unsigned (CdH 199)
Oil on panel, $9\frac{1}{2} \times 6$
Collection Mr and Mrs Germain Seligman, New York
Photo: Brenwasser Studios

174 *Garçonnet Assis*, *c.* 1884
Unsigned (CdH 607)
Conté crayon touched up with gouache, $11\frac{7}{8} \times 9\frac{1}{4}$
Private collection
Photo: courtesy César de Hauke

175 *La Poseuse, de Face*, 1887
Signed l/r (CdH 183)
Oil on board, $10\frac{1}{4} \times 6\frac{3}{4}$
Louvre, Paris
Photo: Giraudon

176 *Femme Assise sous les Arbres*, *c.* 1882
Unsigned (CdH 491)
Conté crayon, $9\frac{11}{16} \times 6\frac{1}{8}$
Formerly owned by Percy M. Turner, London
Photo: courtesy César de Hauke

177 *Condoléances*, *c.* 1886
Unsigned (CdH 655)
Conté crayon, $9\frac{1}{2} \times 12\frac{1}{2}$
Collection César de Hauke, Paris
Photo: courtesy César de Hauke

178 *La Poseuse Debout*, *c.* 1887
Unsigned (CdH 664)
Conté crayon, $11\frac{3}{4} \times 8\frac{7}{8}$
Collection Mr and Mrs Robert Lehman, New York

179 *Le Fourneau*, *c.* 1887
Unsigned (CdH 661)
Conté crayon, $9\frac{1}{4} \times 12$
Louvre, Paris
Photo: courtesy César de Hauke

180 *Une Poseuse Habillée, Buste de Profil*, *c.* 1887
Unsigned (CdH 662)
Conté crayon, $12\frac{1}{2} \times 9\frac{1}{2}$
Destroyed in the fire at the Gare des Batignolles, Paris
Photo: courtesy César de Hauke

181 *Nature Morte (Chapeau et Parapluie)*, *c.* 1887
Unsigned (CdH 663)
Conté crayon with two touches of gouache, $12 \times 9\frac{1}{4}$
Collection Walter C. Baker, New York
Photo: courtesy César de Hauke

182 *La Poseuse de Profil*, 1887
Unsigned (CdH 182)
Oil on board, $9\frac{1}{2} \times 5\frac{7}{8}$
Louvre, Paris

183 *La Poseuse de Dos*, 1887
(CdH 181)
Oil on board, $9\frac{5}{8} \times 6\frac{1}{4}$
Louvre, Paris
Photo: Bulloz

184 *Petite Étude Complète pour 'Les Poseuses'*, 1887
Unsigned (CdH 180)
Oil on panel, $6\frac{1}{8} \times 8\frac{1}{2}$
Private collection
Photo: courtesy César de Hauke

185 *Poseuse Debout, de Face*, 1887
Unsigned (CdH 179)
Oil on board, $10\frac{1}{4} \times 6\frac{1}{4}$
Private collection, Paris
Photo: courtesy César de Hauke

186 *Les Poseuses, Ensemble*, 1888
Unsigned (CdH 184)
Oil on canvas, $15\frac{1}{2} \times 19\frac{1}{4}$
Collection H. P. McIlhenny, Philadelphia
Photo: Charles P. Metts and Son

187 *Les Poseuses*, 1888
Signed l/r (CdH 185)
Oil on canvas, $79 \times 98\frac{7}{8}$
Copyright 1965 the Barnes Foundation

188 *Clowns et Poney, c.* 1887
Unsigned (CdH 668)
Conté crayon, $12\frac{1}{2} \times 9\frac{1}{2}$
Collection Phillips Memorial Gallery,
Washington D.C.
Photo: courtesy César de Hauke

189 *Clowns et Personnages, c.* 1887
Unsigned (CdH 675)
Conté crayon, $9\frac{1}{4} \times 12\frac{1}{4}$
California Palace of the Legion of
Honour
Photo: courtesy César de Hauke

190 *Couple Dansant, c.* 1887
Unsigned (CdH 674)
Conté crayon, $9\frac{3}{4} \times 12\frac{1}{4}$
Collection Mr and Mrs Leigh B. Block,
Chicago
Photo: courtesy César de Hauke

191 *Monsieur Loyal et Poney,* 1887
Unsigned (CdH 669)
Conté crayon, $11\frac{5}{8} \times 8\frac{11}{16}$
Formerly owned by de Hauke and Co.,
New York
Photo: courtesy César de Hauke

192 *Banquistes, c.* 1887
Unsigned (CdH 671)
Conté crayon, $12\frac{1}{4} \times 9\frac{1}{4}$
Private collection
Photo: courtesy César de Hauke

193 *La Parade,* 1887
Unsigned (CdH 681)
Pen-and-ink, $4\frac{13}{16} \times 7\frac{11}{16}$
Collection Baron Robert von Hirsch,
Basle
Photo: courtesy César de Hauke

194 *La Parade,* 1888
Unsigned (CdH 187)
Oil on canvas, $39\frac{3}{4} \times 59\frac{1}{8}$
Metropolitan Museum of Art (Bequest
of Stephen C. Clark, 1960)

195 *L'Avant-Port, Marée Haute à Port-en-Bessin,* 1888
Unsigned (CdH 193)
Oil on canvas, $26 \times 31\frac{7}{8}$
Louvre, Paris
Photo: Eileen Tweedy

196 *Le Pont et les Quais à Port-en-Bessin,* 1888
Signed l/r (CdH 188)
Oil on canvas, $26\frac{3}{8} \times 33\frac{1}{4}$
Collection City Art Museum of St
Louis, Minneapolis

197 *Port-en-Bessin, L'Avant-Port à Marée Basse,* 1888
Signed l/l (CdH 189)
Oil on canvas, $21\frac{1}{8} \times 25\frac{7}{8}$
Collection City Art Museum of St Louis

198 *Entrée de l'Avant-Port à Port-en-Bessin,* 1888
Unsigned (CdH 192)
Oil on canvas, $21\frac{5}{8} \times 25\frac{5}{8}$
Collection Museum of Modern Art,
New York

199 *Les Grues et la Percée à Port-en-Bessin,* 1888
Signed l/r (CdH 190)
Oil on canvas, $25\frac{1}{2} \times 31\frac{3}{4}$
Collection Mr and Mrs Averell Harriman, New York

200 *Port-en-Bessin, Un Dimanche,* 1888
Signed l/l (CdH 191)
Oil on canvas, $25\frac{5}{8} \times 31\frac{7}{8}$
Rijksmuseum Kröller-Müller

201 *Le Pont de Courbevoie, c.* 1887
Signed l/l (CdH 178)
Oil on canvas, $18 \times 21\frac{1}{2}$
Courtauld Institute Galleries
Photo: Eileen Tweedy

202 *Scène de Théâtre,* 1887–8
Unsigned (CdH 683)
Conté crayon, $12\frac{3}{16} \times 8\frac{1}{2}$
Formerly owned by Baronne N.
Gourgaud
Photo: courtesy César de Hauke

203 *La Loge de l'Artiste, c.* 1887
Unsigned (CdH 659)
Conté crayon, $6 \times 9\frac{1}{2}$
Collection Mr and Mrs Richard S. Davis
Photo: César de Hauke

204 *A la Gaité Rochechouart,* 1887–8
Unsigned (CdH 686)
Conté crayon and gouache, $12\frac{1}{8} \times 9\frac{1}{4}$
Fogg Art Museum, Harvard University
Photo: César de Hauke

205 *Au Concert Européen,* 1887–8
Unsigned (CdH 689)
Conté crayon touched up with gouache,
$12\frac{1}{4} \times 9\frac{3}{8}$
Collection Museum of Modern Art,
New York

206 *High C,* 1887–8
Signed u/l (CdH 684)
Conté crayon, $11\frac{5}{8} \times 9\frac{1}{16}$
Formerly owned by Mme Vve Eugène
Rehns
Photo: César de Hauke

207 *Le Chahut*, 1890
Unsigned (CdH 199)
Oil on canvas, 67 1/8 × 55 1/4
Rijksmuseum Kröller-Müller

208 *Le Danseur à la Canne*, 1889–90
Unsigned, cachet l/l (CdH 682)
Conté crayon on cream-laid paper, 11 13/16 × 7 1/8
Formerly owned by Saint, Paris
Photo: César de Hauke

209 *Jeune Femme se Poudrant*, 1890
Signed l/r (CdH 200)
Oil on canvas, 37 1/2 × 31 1/4
Courtauld Institute Galleries

210 *Femme Nue Étendue*, *c.* 1888
Unsigned (CdH 660)
Conté crayon, 9 1/2 × 12 5/8
Formerly owned by Félix Fénéon
Photo: César de Hauke

211 *Paul Alexis*, 1888
Signed l/r (CdH 691)
Conté crayon, 11 13/16 × 9 1/16
Formerly owned by Paul Alexis
Photo: César de Hauke

212 *Étude pour 'Le Cirque'*, 1890
Unsigned (CdH 212)
Oil on canvas, 21 11/16 × 18 1/8
Louvre, Paris
Photo: Eileen Tweedy

213 *Arbres et Bateaux*, 1890
Unsigned (CdH 202)
Oil on board, 6 1/4 × 9 7/8
Collection A. & R. Ball, New York
Photo: courtesy César de Hauke

214 *Étude pour 'Le Chenal de Gravelines, Un Soir'*, 1890
Unsigned (CdH 209)
Oil on board, 6 3/8 × 10
Musée de L'Annonciade
Photo: courtesy César de Hauke

215 *Le Chenal de Gravelines, Un Soir*, 1890
Unsigned (CdH 210)
Oil on canvas, 25 3/4 × 32 1/4
The Museum of Modern Art, New York; gift of the Honorable and Mrs William A. M. Burden, the donor retaining a life interest

216 *Petit Fort-Philippe*, 1890
Unsigned (CdH 699)
Conté crayon, 9 5/16 × 12 3/16
Collection Mme Georges Rehns
Photo: César de Hauke

217 *Le Chenal de Gravelines: Petit Fort-Philippe*, 1890
Signed l/r (CdH 208)
Oil on canvas, 28 3/4 × 36 1/2
Art Association of Indianapolis, Herron Museum of Art

218 *Le Chenal de Gravelines: Direction de la Mer*, 1890
Unsigned (CdH 206)
Oil on canvas, 27 9/16 × 35 7/8
Rijksmuseum Kröller-Müller

219 *Regates à la Grenouillère*, 1890
Unsigned (CdH 705)
Conté crayon, 9 1/16 × 12 1/8
Rhode Island School of Design Museum of Art
Photo: César de Hauke

220 *La Voile Blanche*, 1890
Unsigned (CdH 706)
Conté crayon, 12 3/16 × 9 7/8
Private collection
Photo: courtesy César de Hauke

221 *Le Crotoy, Aval*, 1889
Unsigned (CdH 195)
Oil on canvas, 27 3/8 × 34
Collection Mr and Mrs Stavros Niarchos, Athens

222 *Le Chenal de Gravelines, Grand Fort-Philippe*, 1890
Unsigned (CdH 205)
Oil on canvas, 25 5/8 × 31 7/8
Collection Lord Butler
Photo: John Webb

223 *Le Clown et Monsieur Loyal*, 1890
Unsigned (CdH 710)
Water-colour in blue, red and yellow on tracing paper, 12 × 13 7/8
Louvre, Paris
Photo: courtesy César de Hauke

224 *Le Clown du Premier Plan*, 1891
Unsigned (CdH 712)
Conté crayon, 6 1/8 × 12 3/8
Collection Mme Ginette Signac
Photo: courtesy César de Hauke

225 *Le Cirque*, 1890–91
Unsigned (CdH 213)
Oil on canvas, 73 × 59 1/8
Louvre, Paris

Index

All numbers refer to text pages; those in italic indicate illustrations

Aman-Jean, portrait *34*, 35, 37, *96*
Alexandre, Arsène, 231
Alexis, Paul, 43; portrait *247*
Angrand, Charles, 184
Anquetin, Louis, 184
Apollinaire, Guillaume, quoted 261

Balthus, 266
Baudelaire, Charles, 62
Bellini, 24
Bernard, Emile, 184, 211
Blanc, Charles, 14, 24
Bonnard, Paul, 69
Bonnat, Léon, 249
Braque, Georges, 242
Brunetière, quoted 41

Carolus-Duran, 249
Cézanne, Paul, 30, 247
Chassériau, Théodore, 13
Chéret, Jules, 199, 234, 236, 240, 242, 244, 255, 257
Chevreul, Eugène, 14
Christophe, Jules, quoted 57–8
Clark, Sir Kenneth, quoted 26, 115, 190
Coquiot, Gustave, quoted 146
Corot, Jean-B., 51, 55, 72, 73–4, 106
Costa, Lorenzo, 142; *Allegory 162*, *167*, *168*
Courbet, Gustav, 52, 54
Couture, Thomas, 31
Crane, Walter, *A Fantasy of Fashion, 1837–1887*, 154
Cross, Henri E., 184, 263

Dagnen-Bouveret, 249
Daumier, Honoré, 197, 216
Degas, Edgar, 13, 16, 23, 35, 83, 176, 234, 236, 254
Delacroix, Eugène, 13, 14, 46, 54, 78, 79, 182

Delaunay, Robert, 264, 266
della Francesca, Piero, 24, 122, 266
de Superville, Humbert, 14
Dobrski, Victor (Victor Jozé), 240
Dorra, Henri, 152, 244, 258–9, 260
Dubois-Pillet, Albert, 180, 230, 264
Duchamp, Marcel, 266
Dumaresq, Armand, 9
Dürer, Albrecht, 21

Eluard, Paul, 22
Ernst, Max, 266

Fénéon, Félix, 12, 74, 100, 106, 119, 122, 141, 142, 155, 176–7, quoted 180–1, 184, 201, 206, 210, 218, 226, 230, 231, 242, 258
Finch, Willy, 264
Flaxman, John, 12, 13, 56
Forain, Jean-Louis, 199, 234
Forster, E. M., quoted 157–8
Fry, Roger, quoted 157, 244

Gauguin, Paul, 176, 197, 211, 262
Ghiberti, 24
Giacometti, Alberto, 90
Giorgione, 142
Goncourt brothers, 56, 244
Gris, Juan, 264
Guillaumin, Armand, 176, 199
Guys, Constantin, 199

Helmholz, H., 14
Henry, Charles, 191, 192, 194, 203, *Une Esthétique scientifique* 216, 236, 240, 251, 258, 259, 260
Herbert, R. L., 15, 23, 24, 52, 54–5, 65, 83, 205, 216, 257
Hokusai, 250
Holbein, Hans, 21, 22, 24, 62, 73
Homer, William I., 14, 73, 226
Huysmans, J. K., 56, 146, 176, 234

Ingres, Jean A. D., 13, 24, 25, 62, 65, 70, 71, 73, 201

Janson, H. W., 160, 168
Jozé, Victor, *see* Dobrski

Kahn, Gustav, quoted 30, 58, 184, 194, 218, 234, 236, 249, 262
Kandinsky, Wassily, 107, 266
Klee, Paul, 266
Knobloch, Madeleine, 100, portrait *245, 246,* 249, 262

Lehmann, Henri, 24, 70
Lequien, Justin, 24, 70

Macke, August, 266
Mallarmé, Stéphan, 155, 176
Manet, Edouard, 27, 35
Marey, 242
Marx, Roger, 142
Matisse, Henri, 264, 265, 268
Michelangelo, 13, 24
Millet, Aimée, 68
Millet, Jean-François, 38, 43; *Les Glaneuses 44,* 45–55, 65, 86, 89, 107
Molière, 261
Monet, Claude, 16, 119, 176, 258
Monticelli, Adolph, 250
Moore, George, 176
Moreau, Gustav, 250
Morice, Charles, 42

Pater, Walter, quoted 160, 162
Paulhan, Jean, quoted 176–7
Perugino, 24
Petit, Léonce, 154
Pissarro, Camille, 16, 27, 30, 119, 174, 175, 176; and Lucien, 180, 184; Camille, 185, 197, 206, 210, 216, 218, 230, 231, 262
Pontormo, Jacopo, 24
Poussin, Nicolas, 9, 10, 24, 190
Proudhon, Pierre, 52
Puget, Pierre, 24
Puvis de Chavannes, Pierre, 13, 30, the *Hommage à . . .,* 31, 36; *Doux Pays 36,* 37, 39, 40, 41, 42, 43, 51, 55, 73–4, 124, 142

Quinn, John, 267

Raphael, 13, 24, 71
Rembrandt, 65
Renoir, Auguste, 27, 30, 119, 258
Rewald, J., 152, 157, 177, 230
Rey, Robert, 59, 157
Rimbaud, Arthur, quoted 218, 219
Roger-Marx, Claude, 261
Rood, d'O. N., 14, 45, 57, 73, 74, 75, 119, 181
Rousseau, Theodore, 55

Schapiro, Meyer, quoted 157, 158, 192
Scharf, Aaron, 242
Schuffenecker, Emile, 184
Sensier, A., 44
Seurat, Chrysostome-Antoine (father), 16, portrait *17,* 23, *98*
Seurat, Ernestine (mother), 16, portraits *18, 19*
Severini, Gino, 264
Signac, Paul, 12, quoted 13–16, 58, quoted 59, quoted 65–6, 96, 100, 118, 126, 175, 176, 180, 184, 189, 192, 210, 218, 222, 230, 231, 262, 263
Strindberg, quoted 40
Sutter, David, *Phenomena of Vision* 57

Titian, 24
Toulouse-Lautrec, Henri de, 42, 211, 254

Valéry, Paul, 192
Van de Velde, Henry, 262
Van Gogh, Vincent, 107, 184, 185, 210, 211, 213, 214
Van Rysselberghe, Théo, 184, 263, 264
Verhaeren, 156, 184, 230
Villot, Frédéric, 166–7
Vuillard, Edouard, 19, 69, 96, 197

Whistler, James McNeil, 189
Wind, Edgar, 167
Wittkower, Rudolf, quoted 156

Young, Thomas, 230

Zola, Emile, 56, 146, 247